THOMAS COOK
Travellers

& BRITISH COLUMBIA

VANCOUVER

KU-114-005

AA

Produced by AA Publishing

Written by Carol Baker

Series adviser: Melissa Shales

Copy editor: Eric Inglefield

The Automobile Association would like to thank Robyn Mitchell, Thomas Cook UK.

Edited, designed and produced by AA Publishing.
Maps © The Automobile Association 1993

Distributed in the United Kingdom by AA Publishing, Norfolk House, Priestley Road, Basingstoke, Hampshire, RG24 9NY.

The contents of this publication are believed correct at the time of printing. Nevertheless, the publishers cannot accept responsibility for errors or omissions, or for changes in details given. Assessments of attractions, hotels, restaurants and so forth are based upon the author's own experience and, therefore, descriptions given in this guide necessarily contain an element of subjective opinion which may not reflect the publishers' opinion or dictate a reader's own experiences on another occasion.

We have tried to ensure accuracy in this guide, but things do change and we would be grateful if readers would advise us of any inaccuracies they may encounter.

© The Automobile Association 1993
Reprinted 1996

A CIP catalogue record for this book is available from the British Library.

ISBN 0 7495 0631 8

Published by AA Publishing (a trading name of Automobile Association Developments Limited, whose registered office is Norfolk House, Priestley Road, Basingstoke, Hampshire, RG24 9NY. Registered number 1878835) and the Thomas Cook Group Ltd.

Colour separation: BTB Colour Reproduction, Whitchurch, Hampshire

Printed by Edicoes ASA, Oporto, Portugal

Cover picture: *Downtown Vancouver*
Title page: *Lake O'Hara, Yoho National Park*
Above: *Totem pole, Thunderbirds Park, Victoria*

Contents

Introduction

*B*ritish Columbia, often referred to as BC, joined the Canadian Confederation in 1871, but is still regarded as a youngster in the world community. Yet the life of this Pacific coast province extends a long way back in time, far beyond the birth of this morning's new-born child to the creation of the majestic Coast Mountains, 130 million years ago. The north, with its extremes of temperature, is sparsely populated, while the urban centres of Vancouver and Victoria, where the climate is kind, are attracting more and more people all the time.

The first residents were Asian hunters and berry gatherers, who drifted south along the coast and into the interior around 6000BC. The first visitor to arrive by sea was probably Hoei-Shin, a Chinese Buddhist priest who sailed across the Pacific in AD499.

Although Balboa claimed the Pacific Ocean and all its shores for Spain in 1513, the Spaniards did not settle here until the late 18th century. They stayed only a few years, but left their names: Cardero, Valdez, Juan de Fuca, Bodega y

BC has many provincial parks offering excellent recreation amid superb scenery

Quadra and Malaspina. Explorations by such adventurers as Captain Cook, Alexander Mackenzie, George Vancouver and Simon Fraser resulted in an influx of British settlers, and the area became a British colony in 1858.

Today, ironically, the Asians are back. More than 100,000 Chinese Canadians now live in BC. Other Chinese, both from Hong Kong and Taiwan, are investing in business, real estate and a new way of life in even greater numbers. The Japanese, who already own and manage many businesses in BC, also come by the jetload on holidays, to marvel at the space, the wilderness, the

native culture, and the slopes in Whistler, which they rate among the finest ski resorts of the world.

Vancouver, Canada's gateway to the Pacific, has become a wonderfully cosmopolitan centre, often selecting the best of both European and Asian ways of life and, at the same time, encouraging a rebirth of BC's native Indian cultures.

VANCOUVER QUOTES

'I would not give the bleakest knoll on the bleakest hill of Scotland, for all these mountains in a heap.'
Explorer Captain John Gordon, 1844

*'There's wine in the cup, Vancouver,
And there's warmth in my heart for you.'*
Indian poetess Pauline Johnson, 1911

'You think BC means before Christ. But it doesn't. I'm sitting, wildly surmising, on the edge of the Pacific, gazing at mountains which are changing colour every two minutes in the most surprising way. Nature here is half-Japanese.'
English poet Rupert Brooke, 1913

'British Columbia … If I had known what it was like, I wouldn't have been content with a mere visit. I'd have been born here.'
Canadian humorist Stephen Leacock, 1937

'The history of Canada for about 300 years was a struggle to escape from the wilderness, and for the last half century has been a desperate attempt to escape into it.'
Canadian author Bruce Hutchison, 1953

'Vancouver is one of those cities, like San Francisco, which are victims of their glorious settings. One expects too much of them. As Californians like to say, there is less to them

The beautiful coast at Horseshoe Bay

than meets the eye.'
Travel writer Jan Morris, 1990

'Every single time, when I come back to BC after a trip abroad, I thank my lucky stars I had the common sense to move here early enough in my life to truly appreciate the great natural beauty this province has to offer.'
Merchant banker Peter Thomas, 1991

'In 10 years Vancouver will be an Asian city. About 60 per cent of Vancouver children currently do not speak English or French as their first language. Their native tongues are Cantonese, Mandarin, Japanese, Vietnamese, Korean and other Southeast Asian languages.'
Canadian futurist Frank Ogden, 1991

History

13 June 1792
Captain George Vancouver, exploring the Pacific Coast of North America, enters a body of water he names Burrard's Channel. Today, known as Burrard Inlet, it is the busy Vancouver harbour.

2 July 1808
Simon Fraser, seeking fur-trading routes, arrives at Musqueam at the mouth of the Fraser River, where the native people chase him and his men back upstream.

1846
After a long territorial dispute, a treaty is signed by Britain and the US placing BC firmly in Canada.

2 August 1858
Following the discovery of gold on the Fraser River, American miners begin to pour in. The British Parliament passes an act establishing the mainland colony of BC. The colony of Vancouver Island already exists.

25 November 1858
Colonel Richard Moody arrives with a company of 'sappers' (soldier engineers) and begins building roads. The first road built still exists, as North Road, now the boundary between the Vancouver suburbs of Burnaby and Coquitlam.

26 September 1862
The McCleery family become the first settlers in Vancouver when they occupy land on the north bank of the Fraser on what is now McCleery Golf Course.

October 1862
Three new arrivals from England, John Morton, Samuel Brighouse and William Hailstone file a claim on 500 acres on Burrard Inlet. The land is empty swampy forest, so other colonists laugh-ingly call them 'The Three Greenhorns'. Today that land, the city's apartment-crammed West End, is worth billions.

June 1863
A sawmill, the first industry in the area, is established on the north shore of Burrard Inlet.

30 September 1867
'Gassy' Jack Deighton, so nicknamed because he talked incessantly, builds a saloon in 24 hours with the help of thirsty sawmill workers. The area around his saloon becomes known as Gastown.

1869–70
Gastown gets a jail ... and the name Granville.

20 July 1871
BC joins the Confederation of Canada, formed in 1867.

6 April 1886
The City of Vancouver, renamed from Granville, is incorporated.

13 June 1886
The Great Fire destroys most buildings in the new little city, and 20 people die. Rebuilding begins at once.

23 May 1887
The first Canadian Pacific Railway (CPR) passenger train arrives in Vancouver; Vancouver's growth begins to accelerate.

1902
Vancouver's population reaches 30,000. Charles Woodward opens a department store, still active today.

1904
The Great Northern Railway reaches Vancouver.

1908
The University of BC is founded, which today has 30,000 students.

1913
The World Building is completed, the tallest in the British Empire at the time. Today known as the Old Sun Tower, it looks rather modest.

28 August 1915
The first Canadian Northern Pacific Railway train arrives in Vancouver. Later, the line becomes known as the Canadian National Railway (CNR).

1 November 1919
The CNR Station opens. Today it is the terminal for VIA Rail.

1 January 1929
On amalgamation with two adjacent municipalities, Vancouver's population jumps to 240,000; Canada's third-largest city.

22 July 1931
Vancouver Airport and Seaplane Harbour officially open.

4 December 1936
Vancouver's City Hall opens.

25 May 1939
The third, and present, Hotel Vancouver opens on its present site, just a few days before King George VI and Queen Elizabeth stay in the royal suite. The city names its newest park Queen Elizabeth Park.

6 August 1940
Theatre Under The Stars begins in Stanley Park, and becomes a much-loved tradition.

9 October 1944
The *St Roch,* a vessel operated by the RCMP, arrives back in Vancouver from Halifax, having gone through the Northwest Passage in both directions. Shortly thereafter the *St Roch* sails through the Panama Canal, becoming the first ship to circumnavigate North America.

15 July 1959
Queen Elizabeth and Prince Philip officiate at the opening of the Deas Island Tunnel, now called the Massey Tunnel.

27 April 1965
Yokohama, Japan, becomes a sister city to Vancouver.

10 September 1965
Simon Fraser University opens.

1986
EXPO 86, marking Vancouver's centennial, attracts 21 million visitors during six months and puts Vancouver in the spotlight around the world.

The bright lights of downtown Vancouver stand out at night against the dark shape of Grouse Mountain to the north

Geological Past

*A*bout 130 million years ago, a gigantic upheaval in the earth's crust created the majestic Coast Mountains, the beginning of present-day BC. Sixty-five million years ago, further movements brought forth the Rocky Mountains, and 40 million years later, Cascadia, the Atlantis of the Pacific, sank offshore, leaving Vancouver Island and the Queen Charlotte Islands above sea level. A mere million years ago, most of BC was covered with a blanket of ice 2,500m thick, which slowly began to recede 70,000 years later.

The Fraser River churns over the rapids in its rugged canyon north of Hope

North to south, as the crow flies, Vancouver's terrain runs from mountains down to Burrard Inlet and the low rolling slopes of the city centre, and beyond to the flat fertile delta of the Fraser River, which branches into two arms to greet the sea. Immediately south of the delta lies the American border and Washington State.

It all looks fairly solid, but is actually slowly changing. Vancouverites received a reminder that the earth is alive in 1980, when Mount St Helens in Washington erupted and spewed a film of fine ash over the city. One of Vancouver's most famous landmarks, Siwash Rock in Stanley Park, is the uneroded remnant of a small volcano within the city limits, and black volcanic rock underpins nearby Prospect Point. Volcanic rock was quarried for road material out of the city highpoint that today is Queen Elizabeth Park. Mount Garibaldi, a short drive east, was an active volcano 1,000 years ago.

Indian poet Pauline Johnson, whose ashes were scattered over Siwash Rock, named Lost Lagoon, in Stanley Park, because it used to vanish at low tide, before it was closed in by man.

Nature is continually busy creating, shaping, destroying and displacing, usually at a pace too gentle for mere mortals to detect. At one time a thick layer of ice pressed down over the city; its retreat about 10,000 years ago left the vast and visually delightful panorama of mountains, canyons, fiords, rivers and swamps. Without the weight of the ice, the land lifted, and layers of marine shells have been found several hundred metres above sea-level.

All Fraser River delta land west of New Westminster developed after the ice retreated, and alluvial soils continue to create several metres of new real estate here every year.

A century ago, workers extending Granville Street unearthed ancient tools, weapons and ornaments in the Marpole Midden, the largest of its kind discovered in North America to that date.

A similar midden in Stanley Park provided so many seashells, emptied and discarded by hungry native Indian residents, that park roads were once paved with them.

Constant landslides on to mountain

Osoyoos Lake, BC's warmest freshwater lake, is a mecca for watersports

roads are a regular reminder that geological processes work without pause. Vancouver has even had several minor earthquakes. One in 1946 registered 7.3 at the epicentre, which was fortunately some distance north. But buildings rocked, windows broke and the big clock on the Vancouver Block stopped. Seismologists say Vancouver and environs are very likely to feel the impact of 'The Big One', if and when it comes, although no one will mind if it fails to happen.

Geography

*T*he BC motto, *Splendour Sine Occasu*, which means 'splendour undiminished', is almost an understatement. Canada's most westerly province comprises 950,000 square kilometres of remarkable diverse seascapes and landforms – solitary beaches, quiet coves, primeval rainforests, spectacular fiords, snow-capped ranges, tundra, alpine meadows, glacial lakes, pristine waterfalls, raging rivers and gentle, thermal springs, verdant valleys, plains and deserts.

Each day the sun sets over 6,500 islands, offshore from a rugged 12,000km coastline indented by deep inlets. The magnificent Coast Mountains tower rank after rank in a northwest to southeast alignment. Eastward a broad plateau of rolling range land, mantled with moraines and other glacial deposits, stretches towards the thrusting snowy peaks of the Rocky Mountains. These form a natural barrier between BC and the rest of Canada, which is accessible by land via mountain passes at Crowsnest, Kicking Horse and Yellowhead. Kimberly, located at an altitude of 1,100m is the highest city in the country. North of the Rockies lie the extensive fertile farmlands of the Peace River, a geographical continuation of the prairies.

The Fraser, Skeena, Nass, Stikine, Peace and Columbia rivers weave a web of routes and barriers throughout the province. The earth varies from the silty soil of the Fraser delta and the Okanagan Valley to the barren, lichen-covered lava fields of Terrace. Subterranean volcanic activity produces thermal springs at Harrison, Khalycon, Radium and Fairmont, which are open to the public for warm mineral baths.

Precipitation varies with topography from the permanently damp rainforests of the Queen Charlotte Islands and frequent snowfalls of Mount Robson, the highest peak in the Rockies, to the sunny arid Osoyoos desert with its cactuses, tumbleweed, sagebrush, lizards and rattlesnakes.

Despite BC's vast and varied geography, man has made most areas accessible. A network of paved highways and railway track covers the countryside. The BC ferry fleet, the largest in the world, serves the islands and coastal towns, while in summer luxury liners cruise to and from Alaska along the Inside Passage. International airports at Vancouver and Victoria, 350 other airfields and landing strips, and 100 seaplane bases permit access to remote regions.

Although timber, mining, agriculture and fishing all contribute to provincial coffers, tourism brings in the most revenue. The visitors, who are mostly other Canadians, Americans and Japanese, stay longer on average in BC than anywhere else in the country. What Nature has created, mankind has complemented with almost every conceivable recreational facility, resulting in a remarkable playground, especially in summer. More than 300 land parks and

32 marine parks offer wilderness varying from the 30 alpine lakes and five glaciers of Kokanee Glacier Provincial Park to the colourful underwater world of anemones, abalone and other aquatic creatures sought out by scuba divers along the coast.

In a vibrant city like Vancouver, some people work on Friday, ski on Saturday and sail on Sunday. There is also the possibility of the best in opera, art, theatre, music and cinema on a Saturday evening. As the pulse of the province and centre of commerce and industry, and with its spectacular sea and mountain setting rivalling Hong Kong and Capetown, Vancouver offers just about everything an urbanite could ask for.

BC is a complexity of cultures. The climate is kind in Victoria and Vancouver. Resources are abundant. Yet most of the wilderness remains wilderness.

Emerald Lake reflects the rugged beauty of BC's Rockies in Yoho National Park

Politics

*C*anada is a confederation with parliamentary democracy. The party with the largest number of members elected to Parliament forms the government. In 1992 the Progressive Conservatives were in power, with the Liberals as the next strongest party.

In BC, whose turbulent politics are a source of constant astonishment and amusement to the rest of the country, the New Democratic party is now in control. Other parties include the middle-of-the-road Liberals and the right-wing Social Credit and Progressive Conservative parties. A flamboyant and reckless premier was defeated in 1991, taking most of his party down with him. He was replaced by New Democrat Mike Harcourt, a lawyer who led an ambitious group of candidates to a convincing and significant victory. The ratio of women and of university graduates in the current caucus and in the cabinet is the highest in BC history. Time will reveal the results these liberalising troops will have on the province's fortunes.

The future is challenging. Forestry and its allied industries, which employ 80,000 British Columbians, face ferocious pressure from increasing world competition. Environmentalists, concerned over the future of the forests, are expressing alarm at the brutal cutting, and are convinced that not enough new trees are being planted.

The province's lively political scene is reflected in microcosm in Vancouver, its largest city. For years, left-leaning members of the city council have been engaged in a battle of policy and words with the right, with middle-of-the-road councillors getting flak from both sides. But more recently City Hall has been calming down, with young and competent Mayor Gordon Campbell at the helm.

BC's 19th-century Parliament buildings stand in landscaped grounds by Victoria's Inner Harbour. At night the buildings are outlined by tiny twinkling lights

Culture

*T*here has been an increasing variety of people coming to live in Vancouver during the past few decades, and the resulting mixture has been exhilarating. Immigrants from Hong Kong, Taiwan, Japan, Vietnam and the Philippines in Asia, from Ethiopia, South Africa and Nigeria in Africa, from the US, from many countries in Europe and from Australasia have transformed the city. Little neighbourhoods with a concentration of people from one culture keep popping up. Most of the world is represented by restaurants offering international cuisine and shops selling souvenirs and *objets d'art.*

Vancouver's temperate climate and proximity to nature encourage residents to take off in their pleasure craft, hike or ski the slopes and play tennis and golf whenever possible. For those who like to watch, the BC Lions football team, the Canucks hockey team, and the Canadians baseball team provide alternative excitement.

Vancouver's theatre scene is unpredictable. Smash hits on Broadway do not always translate into successes here, while local plays sometimes become big hits. Dance, once popular, is now in eclipse, although new shows do sometimes pop up.

The Vancouver Opera Association seems to have most success with such popular classics as *Carmen* and *Rigoletto*, featuring visiting guest stars. Such megastars as Pavarotti, however, appear mostly in concert, rather than in local productions.

The Vancouver Symphony is suffering under financial difficulties, but much promise is seen in its new Romanian musical director, Sergiu Commisiona.

The local rock scene is volcanically vigorous, with numerous small groups clamouring for the spotlight. Jazz burns

The Vancouver Symphony Orchestra plays a significant role in BC's cultural life

warmly in a few places, including Café Django and the Alma Street Café.

At the Vancouver Art Gallery, the stately old architecture and the often wild modern art are a powerful mix.

Vancouver also boasts a great public library system and more book stores per capita than any other Canadian city.

Finding your feet

New glass towers crowd older buildings in Vancouver's ever-changing skyline

What to bring

Vancouver has become such a meeting ground of east and west and of business and sports, that almost any wardrobe is acceptable on any occasion. Some women wear fox fur jackets and sandals to the office, while others wear parkas and running shoes. Shorts for both sexes are acceptable leisure wear in summer, but a sweater is often welcome after the sun sets over the Pacific. An umbrella, raincoat and water-resistant footwear can be useful any time of the year, but more so in winter. Layered clothes are practical for venturing up the North

Shore mountains or for boating. Don't worry if you haven't brought everything you need, for practically everything is sold here. Clothes are generally more expensive than in the US, but less expensive than in Europe.

Weather

If grey skies and wet weather bother you, it is better to gamble on the drier and sunnier summer. From November through March, it is often dark and rainy. About 250mm of rain drenches Vancouver in December, compared to 50mm in July. The thermometer hovers around 24°C in July and around 6°C in December. Vancouver snows tend to be light and melt quickly. Winter rain

THE ALIENATING

Mist rolls slowly back up the field
a retreating ghost army
under the mother-of-pearl-ringed
*   moon*
down the wide aisle of massed
trees ragged palisades of sheer
* ·   darkness*
jet against the prickling sky
where stars keep remote counsel
beyond the perimeters of the wind.

Unbending pioneers
wrestled this farm from the forest
broke the deathgrip of stumps
worried the sour dirt arable
danced often in that silvered-roofed
*   barn*
to the fiddle's plangent whine
whirled through squares and circles
when toil stung them hungry for
*   frolic.*

But this is a crueller night and time
we spin to more-cynical music
it hammers its city-spawned
*   rhythms*
against the ribs of the farmhouse
*   behind me*
I crouch in limbo beyond the
*   window lights*
a sudden stranger to both worlds
straining for the thoughts of Sascha
*   the dog*
and Friendly the sheep, chewing his
*   slow dreams.*

Peter Trower

summer. There is less smog than there used to be, now that wood and coal no longer heat homes, but an occasional patch of fog can slow drivers down in autumn. Although a less drastic version of Los Angeles smog lays a thin beige blanket over the city, most visitors find the air refreshing.

Driving on Nelson's steep, broad streets

Driving and parking

More than 80 per cent of the travellers in BC are motorists. Driving is always on the right, with passing on the left. The use of seatbelts is mandatory. Right turns are permitted on red lights, after the vehicle has come to a full stop. City streets, freeways and country roads are well maintained.

Vancouver is becoming more crowded. Rush hour seems to be getting longer and parking downtown more challenging. Many parking meters are restricted during rush hours. There are plenty of big parking lots indoors and out, but on busy days it may take a while to find a space. To Europeans, Vancouver drivers may seem almost archaically sedate, Victorians even more so, although driving manners seem to be deteriorating.

downtown often means snow on the nearby mountains, so skiers can ski all day and evening and still get back downtown for a nightcap. Cool Pacific breezes make seashore strolls pleasant in

Local Customs

Vancouver is an orderly city. People usually queue patiently at bus stops and taxi stands. Pedestrians usually cross at crossings, as they have the right of way at intersections. Drivers rarely honk their horns, even when the traffic is reminiscent of downtown Bangkok at rush hour; it is a ticketable offence.

Canadian couples are used to sleeping in double beds, but many rooms have two beds for the asking.

Vancouverites usually eat salads before the main course, and west coast salads with edible flower blossoms and wild grasses are currently in vogue. Although tastings indicate that BC produces some excellent wines, Vancouverites tend to order imported ones in restaurants. Smoking on the street, once considered bad form, is now common, as most office buildings do not permit smoking, even in lounge areas.

Some of the dour Scots who once settled this area have left a legacy of

Victoria's old Empress Hotel is one of the main highlights of a city bus tour

A RUN THROUGH STANLEY PARK

The cedar hand, wind nodded,
Caressed my arm and sought,
It seemed,
My company.

For greeting or chastisement
At my ungreen intrusion?
Habit fit that path to pounding
*   pace;*

Yet these verdant curtains
May flail my fondness with fret
That I break the filtered, falling
*   shaft*

And sever
The thrust
Too rare in this soft scene.

Bruce I Burnett

The ferry terminal, Granville Island

appearing unapproachable – or maybe it's a remnant of the Wild West, where any stranger was subject to suspicion. Unlike their Seattle cousins, Vancouverites seem reluctant to be the first to say hello, although they usually respond well to friendly people. Although Vancouverites pretend to be puritan at times, the doorman at almost every downtown hotel will accept a $5 tip and keep your car near by for you at no additional charge.

Vancouverites tend to tell other Canadians that it rains all the time here, so that they won't feel so bad about suffering through cold snowy winters, only to be bitten by the mammoth mosquitoes of springtime. On the quiet, most residents of Vancouver admit their city is one of the most beautiful in the world. Few venture into the great outdoors during the dark rainy days of winter, while others jog compulsively right through thunderstorms without losing pace. In the rain, it's a little easier to distinguish the locals; they're usually the ones without umbrellas.

Many visitors find the great patches of wilderness in Greater Vancouver more than adequate for a short visit. But travellers seeking solitude may want to head into the hinterland, where the people are friendlier and Nature's creations are unspoiled.

Stanley Park, Vancouver's green oasis

AREAS OF VANCOUVER

Greater Vancouver is bounded by the
North Shore mountains to the north, the
Strait of Georgia to the west and the
American border to the south. As more
people move to the city, the fertile
farmlands of the Fraser Valley to the east
are fast being replaced by suburban
development.

DOWNTOWN VANCOUVER

In addition to the main business and
shopping area, the city centre has several
different sections. Gastown, the renovated original part of the city, contains
souvenir shops, restaurants and art
galleries. Robson Street has several blocks
of upmarket shops and restaurants
resembling Rodeo Drive in Beverly Hills,

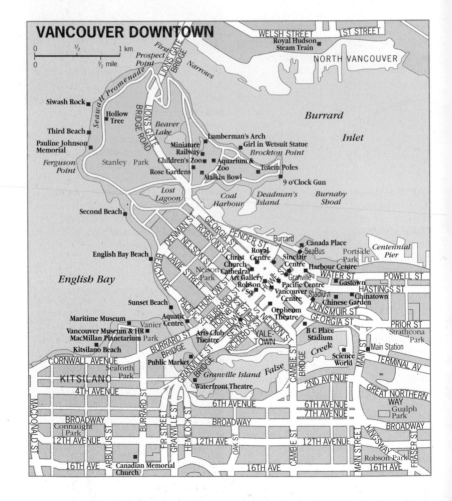

VANCOUVER DOWNTOWN

California. Chinatown has a colourful collection of shops and restaurants especially lively at weekends. Yaletown is an area of old warehouses, recently renovated to house restaurants, galleries and artists, architects and designers.

As a result of large-scale immigration, various ethnic enclaves have developed in Vancouver, and shops and restaurants have opened to cater to their tastes. There are also a lot of East Indians along the southern end of Main Street, Greeks along West Broadway, Germans on Fraser Street, and Italians on Commercial Drive and around Hastings and Nanaimo streets. There is a tiny Japantown on Powell Street and an equally small French-language pocket on West 16th Avenue.

The city's economic watershed is often held to be Cambie Street. To oversimplify, west of that north-south route live physicians, architects, business executives and college professors; east are sawmill workers, waitresses and factory workers.

KERRISDALE

Gentrification in recent years has polished the image of this neighbour-hood, which is now smarter and shinier than Kitsilano to the north.

KITSILANO

Kitsilano, especially along West Fourth Avenue, was once a hotbed of the hippy era, with its pot smokers, tie-dyers, vegetarians, protesters and peaceniks. It is still the most laid-back neighbourhood in town.

SHAUGHNESSY

In this wealthy neighbourhood, streets lined with towering trees curve around imposing mansions. Shaughnessy was established by the Canadian Pacific

Busy traffic in downtown Vancouver is often channelled along one-way streets

Railway a century ago as a residential enclave for executives. In the poorest section, in downtown eastside with Hastings and Carrall streets as its hub, a vigorous group of residents is fighting to improve conditions.

SUBURBIA

Nearly two dozen suburbs surround Vancouver. Richmond, the site of the Vancouver International Airport, is a rapidly growing city to the south. Surrey, a huge municipality on the south side of the Fraser River, is growing rapidly, partly due to the recent extension of the SkyTrain rapid transit. The southern part of Surrey is very attractive, with dairy farms dotted around the green rolling hills.

A quiet, high-income, no-industry residential area, West Vancouver is among the most agreeable suburbs.

AREAS OF BC

BC ROCKIES
This region stretches northwest from the 49th parallel along the Alberta border. The main highway follows the Columbia River through the broad valley of the Rocky Mountain Trench.

CARIBOO CHILCOTIN
This region stretches from the fiords of the Pacific to the forested foothills of the Cariboo mountains.

HIGH COUNTRY
This vast region offers countless lakes, rivers and streams, glaciated mountain passes, waterfalls, dark forests and arid desert plateaux. Sailing, motorboating, canoeing, swimming and windsurfing are other summer pastimes.

KOOTENAY COUNTRY
This region nestles between the fertile farmland of the Okanagan Similkameen and the Rockies.

NORTH BY NORTHWEST
This vast area encompasses one third of BC and stretches from the Rockies across plateaux of forest, lakes and mountain ranges to Haida Gwaii (the Queen Charlotte Islands).

OKANAGAN SIMILKAMEEN
This small, L-shaped region is situated along the American border midway between the Rockies and the Pacific.

PEACE RIVER-ALASKA HIGHWAY
This region is set between the foothills of the Rockies and the Alberta prairie. The Alaska Highway runs from Dawson Creek (Mile Zero) northwest through Fort Nelson and Liard Valley to Alaska.

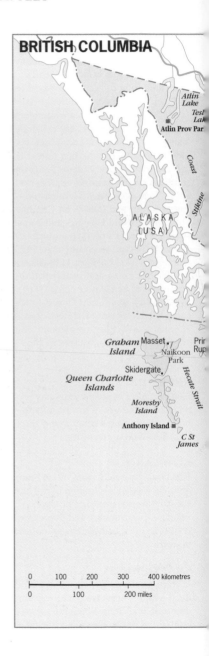

BRITISH COLUMBIA

Atlin Lake
Test Lal
Atlin Prov Par

Coast

ALASKA (USA)

Stikine

Graham Island
Masset
Naikoon Park
Prir Rup

Skidergate
Queen Charlotte Islands

Hecate Strait

Moresby Island

Anthony Island

C St James

0	100	200	300	400 kilometres

0	100	200 miles

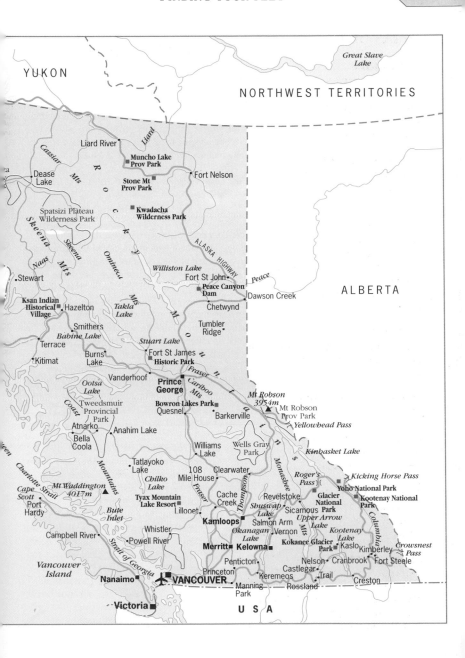

Gastown

Gastown, a five-minute hike from the city centre, is the oldest part of Vancouver. The area was designated a heritage site in 1971. Old gas-style lamps and young maple trees line cobblestoned Water Street, whose three blocks comprise the heart of Gastown. *Allow at least 2 hours*

Begin this tour at the corner of Richards and Water streets. Head east on the north side of Water Street.

Nearby:

Portside Park

Beatles Museum

Vancouver Vocational

Institute

1 THE LANDING

The first stop, The Landing, is an award-winning heritage structure containing a dozen elegant shops clustered around a central lobby, whose arched floor-to-ceiling window frames the North Shore mountains. A shiny escalator leads from one polished oak floor to the other. Head to the lower level, pick up a local newspaper or the *New York Times* at the Fleet Street news-stand and savour a cappuccino and muffin, a good mélange of America and Europe, at the adjacent L'Express Café or the 1950s-style diner at the east end of the building.

Landmark shops sell Scottish tartans, Belgian chocolates, Japanese lingerie, cut and potted flowers, Canadian winter clothes, gold jewellery handcrafted on site, designer clothes and toys for children, embroidered Victoria cushions, maple wood salad bowls and smoked salmon packed for shipping.

Continue along Water Street.

2 INUIT GALLERY

Water Street is lined with dozens of shops selling everything from souvenir sweat-shirts to art deco furniture. The most exciting stop is the Inuit Gallery, a few doors east of The Landing which houses an impressive array of Inuit sculpture and northwest native art. The so-called naive art recalls the way Inuit families used to live in harmony with their harsh land, expressed in soapstone and whalebone sculptures. The shop also sells northwest native Canadian cedar carvings, buttoned blankets and ceremonial masks.

The delightful steam clock is a notable landmark along Gastown's Water Street

A little further along on the left is the steam clock.

3 STEAM CLOCK
Dedicated to the citizens of Vancouver in 1977, the steam clock was built by Gillett & Johnston of Croydon, England. The movement was based on an 1875 vintage design and has a 19kg gold-plated pendulum. A machine in a nearby basement is triggered by the clockwork every 15 minutes and little pins play a Westminster Chimes tune which electronically blows the steam whistles. The steam manifold for the five whistles sits on top of the cube housing the four dials, each highlighted by four enamelled copper dogwood flowers. A 24-carat gold-plated frame surrounds the dials which glow at night.
Continue along Water Street.

4 THE COURTYARD
In the next block meander through The Courtyard where Vancouver architects, tour operators and lawyers work behind huge glass windows. The outdoor café and delicatessen up the stairs provides a pleasant pause and a view across the harbour.
At the end of Water Street turn right into Carrall Street.

5 MAPLE TREE SQUARE
In Maple Tree Square stands the statue of 'Gassy' Jack Deighton, a garrulous Yorkshireman who built a saloon for lumber mill workers on the site of the Broghes building behind in 1867. The building is made with bricks from China used as ballast on sailing ships calling for timber at the Hastings Mill. Deighton, who had arrived in Vancouver with his wife, six dollars, a few sticks of furniture and a yellow dog, was an overnight success. Because he was so talkative and optimistic about prospects for Burrard Inlet, locals called him 'Gassy Jack,' and the ramshackle collection of huts and shops surrounding the saloon was dubbed Gastown. The name stayed, although the city grew westward and changed its name to Vancouver. Jack's statue faces the old Europe Hotel, a good example of the renovated Victorian buildings in Gastown.
Turn west through the Gaoler's Mews.

6 GAOLER'S MEWS
This cobblestoned courtyard is where Vancouver's first gaol once stood. A little further along, Blood Alley marks the site of many dastardly deeds during the settlement of the Wild West.

The south side of Water Street is also lined with shops and restaurants. Water Street restaurants cover the cuisines of Italy, France, Kenya, India and America. One of the best stops for lunch is Umberto's Al Porto, whose downstairs replicates a Tuscan farmhouse and whose upstairs provides a panoramic sweep of railcars carrying Canadian wheat and containers, backdropped by helicopters landing at the heliport in front and the SeaBus shuttling back and forth to North Vancouver.
Return along Water Street to The Landing.

Chinatown

Vancouver's Chinatown, the second largest in North America (at present) after San Francisco, crams a lot of life into six city blocks, a 10-minute walk from city centre (see page 49). *Allow two hours for walking and another hour for dim sum (see pages 166–7)*

Begin this tour at the southwest corner of Carrall and Pender streets.

Nearby:

Church of China

Sun Tower

1 SAM KEE BUILDING

The Sam Kee Building is the narrowest building in the world (1.8m by 30m), and is listed in the *Guinness Book of Records*. The two-storey building, once living quarters for a Chinese family, is now home to Jack Chow Insurance and a group of architects upstairs who own the building.

2 CHINESE CULTURAL CENTRE

In the next block east, the Chinese Cultural Centre, marked by an enormous red gateway, houses a library and rooms for language lessons, tai chi, Chinese painting, lantern making and frequently changing exhibits of Oriental and Canadian art. *Behind the CCC lies the Dr Sun Yat-sen Park and Garden.*

3 DR SUN YAT-SEN PARK AND GARDEN

High whitewashed walls hide this pocket of peace from the bustling city beyond. Modelled after the classic scholars gardens of the Ming Dynasty (1368–1644), the Taoist balance of yin and yang (light and shadow, smooth and rough, large and small) creates perfect harmony. This quiet, secluded sanctuary shelters varied vistas of pebbled patios, moon gates, lattice windows, see-through shrubbery, placid milky-jade pools and craggy grey limestone. *Cross East Pender Street.*

4 EAST PENDER STREET

Across East Pender Street, the Wing
Sang Building, housing the Yen Lock
Restaurant, is the oldest structure in
Chinatown, dating from 1889.

Both sides of Pender are lined with
Mandarin, Cantonese and Szechwan
restaurants, and shops selling such
imported goods as wickerware, parasols
and porcelain, bamboo bird cages and
jade jewellery. Prices are reasonable, but
browsers are welcome. At the Chinese
pharmacies, it is intriguing to watch the
experts mixing potions of herbs, ginseng
root, dried cuttlefish, powdered antler
velvet and other exotic ingredients for
infusions to alleviate everything from
influenza to impotence. Many westerners
now take ginseng and royal jelly.
Continue east along East Pender Street.

5 LITTLE JAPAN

At 173 East Pender, down a few stairs,
is a cluster of small shops called Little
Japan. Kimono Corner artfully displays
traditional Japanese clothing and *noren*
(cotton door hangings). The grocery
store is highlighted by shelves of

*The Dr Sun Yat-sen Garden, a taste of the
Orient in Vancouver's Chinatown*

chocolate Pocky's, a hit with children
from any country. A restaurant serves
sushi, teriyaki, soba and other
specialities, along with take-out bento
box lunches. Another area displays
Japanese pottery, porcelain, lacquerware,
cards and books.
*Cross Main Street, still on East Pender
Street, turn right on Gore Avenue, walk a
block to Keefer Street and turn right again.*

6 KEEFER STREET

Here the predominant aroma announces
windows of Chinese pastries. Most
pastry shops have a room at the back for
a tasty cup of tea and a snack (the coffee
is usually mediocre). On the south side
of Keefer stands a shopping centre, with
Hon's Wun-tun House (great soup and
noodles for low prices; cash only, no
alcohol) at street level. The big
supermarket in the basement is not
nearly as much fun as street shopping.
*Follow Keefer Street two blocks west back to
the Dr Sun Yat-sen Park and Garden.*

Chinese Canadians

During the 5th century, several Chinese Buddhist priests visited a country they called Fu Sang, now believed to have been the west coast of Canada. But the first real wave of Chinese immigrants did not arrive until the 1856 gold rush. Some stayed and started farms and laundries or worked in the salmon canneries, sawmills and coal mines. Some 25 years later, 10,000 Chinese workers were imported to lay track for the cross-Canada railway. Racism forced Chinese families to live crowded together in a small area, the beginning of today's Chinatown in Vancouver. Now more than 150,000 Chinese Canadians live all over the city, and others have settled elsewhere in the province.

Although 50 per cent of newcomers to BC are from other Canadian provinces, about 15,000 Asian immigrants have been arriving each year. Most of the people arriving from Hong Kong and Taiwan bring considerable wealth, skills, willingness to work, and sophistication.

Some Chinese come here because they like the space, the cleanliness, the order and the economic opportunities. Many Hong Kong families, concerned about Hong Kong's return to China in 1997, send their teenagers to study in Canadian schools and universities, to provide them with more career opportunities. Others are investing capital in property, manufacturing, electronics and other ventures in BC so that they might take up residence here later on.

Fortunately, the descendants of the original British settlers in BC are developing greater tolerance of other races. Although about 25 per cent of children entering school here speak Cantonese or Mandarin as their mother tongue, young Vancouverites are no longer concerned whether their friends are of Asian or European background. The highest office in the province, that of lieutenant-governor, is today held by David Lam, a Chinese immigrant, who is highly respected and admired.

Vancouver's Chinese community greets the New Year with exciting parades, elegant dances and colourful costumes

Granville Island

Granville Island is actually a peninsula. Once a swampy tidal flat and later the industrial heart of Vancouver, these 15 hectares of land are now an urban oasis of parks and walkways and renovated warehouses, transformed into a successful combination of more than 200 commercial, cultural, recreational and industrial enterprises. *Allow about two hours plus extra time for more leisurely browsing and a meal.*

Nearby:

Aquatic Centre

Waterfront Theatre

Walk south from downtown for 10 minutes to the foot of Hornby Street or the Aquatic Centre and take the five-minute mini-ferry ride across False Creek. There is complimentary three-hour parking for both cars and boats on the island.

1 ART CLUB THEATRES

Overlooking the ferry terminal are two Arts Club theatres. Walk right between them to the Information Centre which has maps, a calendar of current events and other brochures, and offers an audio-visual presentation explaining the evolution of the area.

Northwest is the Public Market, well worth a stroll through,

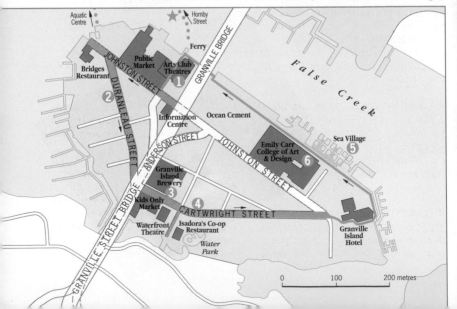

if only to enjoy the aroma of a great array of local and imported fruits and vegetables, fish and seafood, plants and flowers and fast food stands. On the waterfront, a bevy of buskers, including colourful clowns and jugglers and sometimes mediocre musicians, entertain benches of visitors munching such market products as Vietnamese salad rolls and Italian lasagne.

Northwest of the market is a good place to watch the yachts and motor boats slip out to English Bay beyond. The deck at Bridges Restaurant (there may be a queue) is a super spot to sit in the sun or watch the sunset.
Turn south into Duranleau Street.

2 DURANLEAU STREET

Duranleau Street sports a series of maritime shops selling rugged outdoor wear, scuba gear, yacht fittings and other nautical wares. Across the street, the Net Loft shelters a dozen shops, including Edie's Hats with a selection of stylish headgear; The Postcard Place; Paper Ya's which features handmade writing paper and other paper art from around the world; Mesa, where a weaver may be at work at the loom; and the Wickaninnish Gallery of native jewellery and sculptures.
Cross Anderson Street.

3 GRANVILLE ISLAND BREWERY

Across Anderson Street, the Granville Island Brewery produces a popular preservative-free light lager (Bavarian-style pilsner) and features free tastings every afternoon.
Cross over to Cartwright Street.

4 CARTWRIGHT STREET

The Kids Only Market houses two dozen shops and activity areas, and a playcare centre for pre-schoolers. Just beyond the

Waterfront Theatre is the supervised summertime Water Park, where children douse each other with revolving water canons, while parents watch over a coffee or lunch at adjacent Isadora's, a co-operative, reasonably-priced restaurant which has a children's play area inside for rainy days.

The rest of Cartwright Street is lined with art studios, galleries and craft shops, and leads east to the Granville Island Hotel.
Continue east to the Granville Island Hotel and the Sea Village.

5 SEA VILLAGE

On the north shore, near a big rusting crane overhead, is a fleet of floating homes, many with skylights and patios hidden with plants and flowers. The Sea Village is a private residential complex, but walk part way down the ramp to see the colourful collection of rural mailboxes.
Continue along the boardwalk northwest to the Emily Carr College of Art & Design.

6 EMILY CARR COLLEGE OF ART & DESIGN

Here, big windows reveal students at work. Visitors are welcome to view the student art exhibits in the foyer. Next door is the Ocean Cement factory, which somehow seems to belong and makes the area more interesting. Beyond a few more craft shops along the shore is the ferry dock.

Active visitors can sign up for classes at the art studios, enjoy a reading from West Coast Psychics above the Arts Club Lounge, go parasailing over English Bay, or rent a one- or two-seater kayak to paddle up False Creek past the floating homes to the Science Centre.
Return to the ferry.

Art in Public Places

Vancouver has a young but flourishing art scene, resulting in more and more interesting art in public places. *Allow about 2 hours*

Nearby:

Holy Rosary

Cathedral

Beatles Museum

Begin at the Royal Bank of Canada at 1025 Georgia Street.

1 ROYAL BANK OF CANADA

At the top of the escalator in the main lobby is the 'Ksan Mural, nine panels of glowing red cedar and outlined in red, black and turquoise to depict the exploits of the raven in native Canadian mythology. It took six carvers three months to create this 35m-long masterpiece. The carvers are from 'Ksan (which means 'between the banks'), a native village reconstructed near Hazelton, BC, on a site where native villages have existed for 7,000 years. *Continue east along Georgia Street.*

2 CATHEDRAL PLACE

At Cathedral Place, 925 West Georgia, the next block east, take

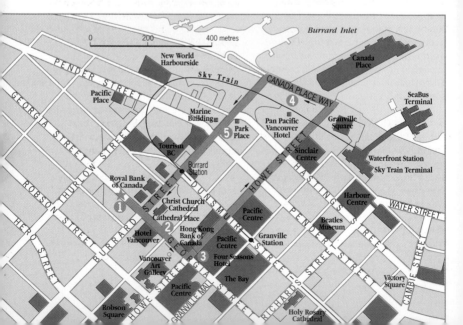

time to watch the tinkling brass pipes and fractured glass of 'Navigational Device' respond to the movement of people present in the foyer. This imposing sculpture, created by local artist Robert Studer, is based on a navigation aid found in the Queen Charlotte Islands. The hieroglyphics etched on the glass resemble oriental language characters but are undecipherable.
One block east is the Hong Kong Bank of Canada.

3 HONG KONG BANK OF CANADA

The next stop is the Hong Kong Bank of Canada at 885 West Georgia, one block east. The impulse to duck is almost irresistible as the 30m-long shining pendulum swings smoothly through the air just 4m overhead. Suspended 30m above the atrium floor, the buttress aluminium column blends briefly with a matching buttress on the floor before reversing its swing. The pendulum, sculpted by British Columbian Alan Storey, seems to form the workings of some wonderful stylised clock. The atrium café (smoking not permitted) is a pleasant place to enjoy a cappuccino and the soothing hypnotic rhythm of the giant pendulum.

Right across the street is a fabulous fountain, framed by the elegant columns and sweeping steps of the Vancouver Art Gallery, designed as a courthouse in 1907 by Victoria architect Francis Rattenbury. The fountain was built in 1966 to commemorate the union of the crown colonies of BC and Vancouver Island. A vivid mosaic of blue, turquoise, gold and green forms a wave-like pattern in the pool around a column of rough-hewn rock.
Walk five blocks north on Howe Street.

4 PAN PACIFIC VANCOUVER HOTEL

The public rooms of this waterfront hotel, at 999 Canada Place Way, house a rich diversity of watercolours, oil paintings and prints. In the lobby, a 3m-high vellum map celebrates the third (1790) and final voyage of Captain Cook to Vancouver. A series of whale sculptures overlook the reception desk, and elsewhere flamboyant abstracts, bright still lifes and glorious landscapes share wall space with antique saris, northwest native art, antique maps and etchings.
Walk along the waterfront to Burrard Street, then south to Hastings Street.

5 PARK PLACE

Park Place, a glowing pink glass highrise at 999 Hastings Street, features a colourful collage of tactile woven strips echoing the busy Vancouver harbour scene with water, boats, buildings and mountains. Across Burrard Street stands the Marine Building, which was constructed on the eve of the Great Depression at the then-stupendous cost of $2.5 million. For a decade, this art deco structure was the tallest building in the British Commonwealth. Intricate art inside and out emphasises marine transportation. Terracotta insets on the façade depict trains, planes and zeppelins. Brass strippings of such marine creatures as seahorses and octopuses frame the doors. Lobby walls in sea green and gold feature ship prows jutting out, waves billowing beneath and full sails above. On a sunny day, light filters through a stained-glass fanlight to illuminate a marble mosaic of the zodiac on the lobby floor.
Continue south along Burrard Street to the start of the walk.

Trolley Tour

The Trolley Tour (tel: 255–2444) is the best preview of Vancouver's varied attractions. The four bright red and gold non-polluting gas-operated trolleys, decorated in oak and brass, are replicas from the 1890s. You may jump off and explore at any of the 17 stops and then catch the next trolley. *Allow at least 2 hours*

Tours run from 09.00–16.00hrs at 30-minute intervals from April to October.

The tour begins in historic Gastown at the two-tonne **Steam Clock** (**1**), which operates on steam generated from the heating system of a nearby building. The clock whistles every quarter hour and spews out wreaths of steam on the hour (see page 23). The trolley travels northwest along cobblestoned Water Street past the old CPR Station, now the SeaBus terminal, to the soaring canvas sails of **Canada Place** (**2**), the city convention centre and cruise ship berth for some of the most luxurious craft in the world.

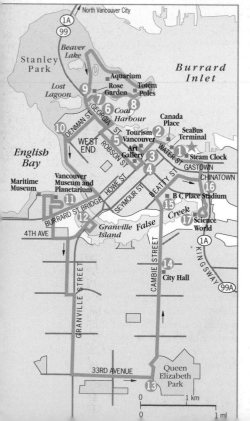

Next stop is **Tourism Vancouver** (**3**), to stock up on brochures about local attractions and events. The tour wheels past the **Vancouver Art Gallery** (**4**) in Hornby Street, the elegant restaurants and boutiques of **Robson Street** (**5**) and then follows **Georgia Street** (Coal Harbour – **6**) west to watch gaggles of Canada geese preening on grassy lawns and float planes skimming forests of masts in the marina as they take off for Vancouver Island and the Sunshine Coast.

Stanley Park, which juts out into English Bay, has three stops. At the **Aquarium** (**7**), Canada's largest, there are orcas, belugas, otters and other aquatic residents.

The next stop is the **Totem Poles** (**8**), a stunning array of native carvings, backdropped by a breathtaking view across the four floating fuel stations of

Coal Harbour to Canada Place. The last park stop is the **Rose Garden (9)**, near Georgia Street, with 300 species of roses, many prized for their perfume and colour.

The trolley heads southwest through the densely-populated West End, a cluster of skyscrapers looking across **English Bay (10)** and Georgia Strait to where the sun sets on the mountains of Vancouver Island.

The route crosses the Burrard Street Bridge to the star-studded Planetarium and the **Vancouver Museum (11)** in Chestnut Street, housing a huge array of artefacts which illustrate the settlement of the West Coast.

Granville Island (12), once decaying warehouses, has now been transformed into an area of theatres, art galleries, shops, restaurants, waterside walkways and a huge indoor market, featuring everything from fudge and fine art to fortune tellers.

The next stop is **Queen Elizabeth Park (13)**, formerly two stone quarries but now attractive colourful gardens, a popular venue for local weddings. Little Mountain (152m), in the middle of the park, is the highest point in the city.

Heading downtown again, the trolley pauses at **City Hall (14)**, an art deco building surrounded by woods and swamp when it was built in 1936.

The next stop is **BC Place Stadium (15)**, reminiscent of a gigantic marshmallow, which sports one of the world's largest air-supported domed roofs.

In **Chinatown (16)**, the trolley passes outdoor displays of exotic fruits and vegetables and shop windows crowded with rattan, bamboo and brass. Golden dragons top streetlight lanterns, pagoda roofs cap phone booths and

A gardener's delight – Queen Elizabeth Park is a riot of colour in summer

street signs are in both English and Cantonese.

The last stop is **Science World (17)**, a sparkling silvered 17-storey geodesic sphere built for EXPO 86, which is a hands-on science museum with changing exhibits and one of the largest OMNIMAX theatres in the world.

The tour ends back at the steam clock in Gastown.

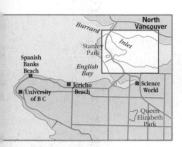

A Boat Ride on a Bus

The SeaBus runs every 15 minutes from 06.00 – 18.00hrs and at half-hour intervals during the evening; reservations not required. The crossing takes about 15 minutes.

Allow 2 hours

The SeaBus provides an inexpensive harbour cruise, along with a great opportunity to explore Lonsdale Quay and Waterfront Park in North Vancouver.

Start this tour at the SeaBus Terminal, located at the north end of Granville Street.

1 SEABUS TERMINAL

Tall creamy pillars mark the entrance to this classic old brick building. The beautifully renovated interior of the terminal showcases a series of paintings from 1916 of the Rocky Mountains, looking down on a large lobby surrounded by several shops, fast-food stops and coffee bars.

Pause briefly on the overhead ramp *en route* to the SeaBus to watch railcars being shunted ahead and back over the shining rails, as trains load and unload. Then board the SeaBus for the sail across the inner harbour. The original ferry that linked

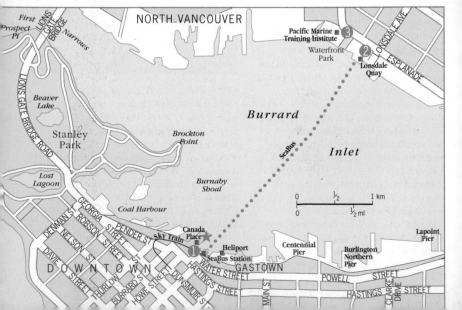

Vancouver with the North Shore in 1900
took considerably longer. The SeaBuses,
appropriately named the SS *Beaver* and
the SS *Otter,* have no outside decks, but
the windows provide a maritime pastiche
of freighters with many foreign flags,
luxury cruise ships sailing to and from
Alaska, a variety of smaller pleasure craft,
and float planes taking off and landing.

North looms the imposing majesty of
the Coast Range, west the forest green
peninsula of Stanley Park and the Lions
Gate Bridge. Southward stand the
shining sails of Canada Place and the
mirrored highrises of downtown, in
sharp contrast with an eastward-
stretching line of old buildings huddled
along the waterfront. At night the dark
waters reflect the city lights.

After disembarking on the North Shore, turn
right to Lonsdale Quay.

2 LONSDALE QUAY

The ground floor of this airy glass and
steel structure, right at the water's edge,
features a public market with a colourful
assortment of local and imported fruit
and vegetables, meat and fish, breads
and pastries, cut and dried flowers and
potted plants. Inexpensive fast-food
restaurants serve everything from Italian
pizza to Vietnamese salad rolls. A snack,
a coffee or a cold drink on the outside
deck includes the stunning harbour view
at no extra charge. The second level has
a charming collection of gift shops and
boutiques, while the third level is the
entrance to the Lonsdale Quay Hotel.

West from the Quay and the SeaBus
Terminal lies Waterfront Park.

3 WATERFRONT PARK

A leisurely stroll along the meandering,
wide paved walkway takes about half an
hour. Along the seawall, signs identify

The SeaBus ferry plies Burrard Inlet

prominent downtown buildings. A short
wooden pier with a covered (it does rain
here occasionally!) observation deck and
benches juts out over the water. During
the short months of summer, musical
concerts are held here on many Sunday
afternoons and, at other times local clubs
enjoy kite-flying, square dancing, vintage
car shows and native Pow-wows. A
noticeboard at the west end of the park
lists events, dates and times.

Beside the walkway stands a huge
series of irregular, separate steel arches
spanning a shrub-covered gully, a
modernistic sculpture entitled *Cathedral*
by artist Douglas Senft. A little further
west, an elegant stylised sundial
dominates Sailor's Point Plaza. The base
of the sculpture contains tiny sketches of
sunken ships. The plaza is dedicated to
people who have lost their lives at sea in
both peace and wartime. A plaque on the
plaza celebrates Captain George
Vancouver, the European who
discovered and named Burrard Inlet.

Before heading back, peek through
the windows of the Pacific Marine
Training Institute, to see the assembly of
boats, ropes, outboard engines and other
nautical devices used by modern
mariners in training.

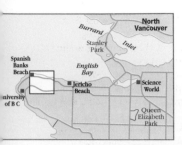

Pacific Spirit Park

A walk in the wild woods on the edge of the city offers patches of ocean framed by red cedars where squirrels scuffle through the underbrush, birds sing and serenity is all around – just a few of the pleasures of Pacific Spirit Park. Park personnel working on the trails are also helpful. *Allow about 2 hours, plus time for birdwatching*

The park is about a 20-minute drive from downtown; count on half an hour by bus (no 4). Maps are available at the park information office on West Sixteenth Avenue and at information boards at many trailheads.

Begin at Chancellor Boulevard, where the extra lane for parking begins, just beyond the Pacific Spirit Park sign. Start on the Pioneer Trail, then follow the first right to the Spanish Trail, which meanders through the woods to Spanish Banks beach or loops back on to the Pioneer Trail to the entrance.

The Pioneer and Spanish trail loop, which is about 2km long, can be muddy in sections, but this is to be expected in a rainforest. The Spanish Trail heads north into tall trees and undergrowth and for a while parallels the south edge of a tree-choked ravine. A few metres off the trail, walkers can peer down into its leafy depths.

Just a few minutes into this forest, traffic sounds fade, sunlight filters through branches overhead, and the aroma of earth and cedar fills the air. Lush ferns, salal, holly and salmonberry bushes line the trails. Spiders' webs glisten and mushrooms cluster on fallen trunks. An occasional woodpecker drums on rotting trees, and tiny wrens and juncos flit about. A chipmunk scurries down a Douglas fir and sometimes frogs serenade. Although racoons, weasels, skunks, otters and foxes make their homes in the undergrowth, they are usually shy when people are around.

Where the trail slopes down sharply and becomes rougher, it soon divides. The Spanish Trail heads steeply downhill and north to Spanish Banks beach, soon visible through the trees. The Pioneer Trail turns west, through a wooden gate.

Climb over a fallen tree trunk to an open glade called the Plains of Abraham. At the turn of the century, a John Stewart ran a dairy farm here, but the once visible

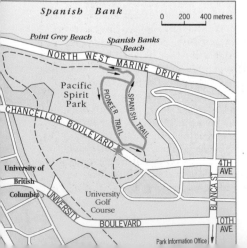

foundations have now become overgrown with fireweed and blackberry bushes. A sign to the southwest indicates the Pioneer Trail, the corduroy road built by Stewart so he could haul his milk to market.

For a longer walk, cross the western edge of the clearing and follow the winding trail north to the cliff edge, where it swings west to parallel the cliff tops and provide views of Burrard Inlet and the North Shore Mountains. The trail eventually ends at a clearing on

North West Marine Drive across from the beach. Any blue herons flying overhead are probably returning to their homes hidden in these woods.

Some 34 trails meander 53km through Pacific Spirit Park. All that is needed is a map and a reasonable sense of direction.

Several trails begin across from the park information office. Many are popular with dog walkers, horseback riders, joggers, hikers and mountain bikers. Film makers occasionally adapt the park for sets, varying from the Amazon jungle to rural Pennsylvania.

Fishing boats at Burrard Inlet

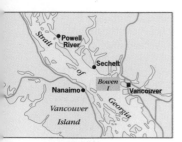

Island Walk

Bowen Island is a wonderful day trip from
Vancouver. This lush, green bowl-shaped isle,
capped by 760m Mount Gardner, has long been
a holiday hideaway for Vancouverites. From
downtown Vancouver, take the Blue Bus
(tel: 985–7777) on Georgia Street, which runs

Most visitors arrive

aboard BC Ferries

Howe Sound Queen

tel: 685–1021.

every half-hour to Horseshoe Bay. Allow an hour for the
bus trip. Bus no 250 follows scenic Marine Drive through
West Vancouver and bus no 257 follows the highway.
Allow a day for the trip

By car the drive takes half an hour; head northwest along
Georgia Street, across the Lions Gate Bridge and follow the

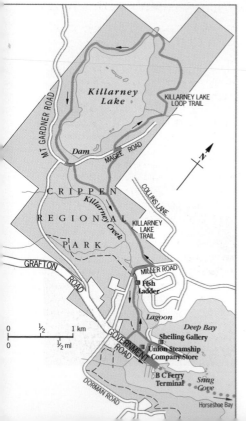

ferry signs west along the Upper Levels
Highway. There is usually ample parking
in Horseshoe Bay, except on holiday
weekends. Since a car is not necessary
on the island, board the ferry as a foot
passenger.

As the ferry rounds the point from
Horseshoe Bay into Queen Charlotte
Sound, the Lions and the Howe Sound
Crest mountains appear dramatically
outlined against the sky. South across
the water lies little Passage Island, Point
Atkinson lighthouse and, across English
Bay, Point Grey.

From the ferry dock in Snug Cove,
it is a three-minute walk along
Government Road to the commercial
centre of the island: a couple of pubs,
restaurants with flower-decked patios,
craft shops, bakeries and the restored
Union Steamship Company Store, now
the local library and post office. A large
map of the island stands on the grass
in front.

Detour right before the store where
a short tree-lined road leads to a freshwater lagoon on one side and the calm
waters of Deep Bay on the other. Just

before the lagoon, a right turn on Cardena Drive leads to the Sheiling Gallery, where artist Sam Black finds models for his wonderful bird watercolours right in his own back yard.

Opposite Cardena Drive, a green sign indicates a leafy trail that marks the entrance to Crippen Regional Park and the Killarney Lake Trail, which is a 6km round trip. The trail is wide and fairly flat, except for a few steep sections. For a leisurely stroll, allow about two hours.

A few minutes along the trail the sound of plunging Terminal Creek announces two fish ladders zigzagging up the rocky hillside beside the creek. During October and November salmon that went to sea after being raised in a nearby hatchery return after two or three years to leap the ladders upstream to spawn in the waters they came from.

The trail, flanked by leafy screens of trees, emerges on to Miller Road. About 100m to the right, the trail continues on the other side. A second-growth forest of red cedar, hemlocks and maples towers

From Horseshoe Bay it is a short ferry ride to Snug Harbour on Bowen Island

over a tangled undergrowth where huge stumps bear silent witness to earlier logging.

The trail crosses Magee Road to the Killarney Lake Loop Trail, where bikes and horses are not allowed. The main trail heads north around the lake to a gravel beach with picnic tables, washrooms and a small swimming area. The trail climbs slightly to join a broad boardwalk over a marsh where Labrador tea, bog laurel, sweet gale bushes and the carnivorous sundew plant thrive. In early summer brilliant yellow skunk cabbage, which smells like it sounds, glows in the underbrush. Blue herons hunch patiently in the shallow water waiting for dinner to swim by. The trail meanders on, with frequent views of the lake and the forested foothills around Mount Gardner. Follow the signs back to Snug Cove to catch the ferry back to the mainland.

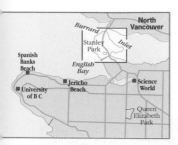

Cycling the Seawall

The Stanley Park Seawall must be one of the best urban cycle routes in the world. About 150 benches line the seawall. Several shops near the Georgia Street entrance to the park, a 10-minute walk from most downtown hotels, rent bicycles and tandems by the hour. The 10km-long paved pathway follows the perimeter of the 400-hectare peninsular park. The right side of the pathway, which is mostly level, is set aside for cyclists. The trail runs counter-clockwise and begins at Lost Lagoon. Walk bikes along the underpass and right to the seawall. *Allow about 2 hours*

1 VANCOUVER ROWING CLUB
Just past Km 0 is the Tudor-style Vancouver Rowing Club. Single skulls and eights skim Coal Harbour's sheltered waters where coal was discovered in the 1800s. Across the harbour,

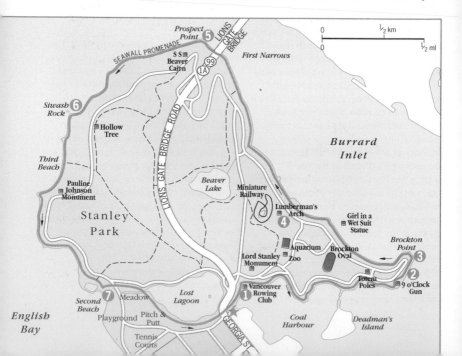

the city skyline is highlighted by the big white canvas sails of Canada Place. Almost opposite the Rowing Club stands a statue of Lord Stanley, a former Governor-General of Canada, who in 1889 dedicated the park 'to the use and enjoyment of people of all colours, creeds and customs for all time'.

2 NINE O'CLOCK GUN

A little further along stands a statue of Scottish poet Robert Burns and another of Harry Jerome, once the world's fastest runner. The Nine O'Clock Gun, which once called herring fishermen home, still booms across the harbour every evening.

3 BROCKTON POINT

A bright red and white striped lighthouse marks Brockton Point, where fishermen cast their lines. Across Burrard Inlet brilliant yellow piles of sulphur await export. Behind lies Brockton Oval, a cinder jogging track encircling a summer cricket pitch which in winter is used by rugby players. A little further along, the bronze sculpture of a *Girl in a Wetsuit* sits in the water near the shore, backdropped by the elegant sweeps of the Lions Gate Bridge. Although many residents initially found her frivolous, she is now widely accepted and admired.

4 LUMBERMAN'S ARCH

At Lumberman's Arch, about Km 3, grassy slopes overlook a water park for children. This was once the site of a Squamish native village and tons of seashells from the midden were used to surface the first road in the park in 1888. It is a short cycle off the seawall to the aquarium and zoo (see pages 78–9). Fishermen wait hopefully beside the huge pillars that support the Lions Gate Bridge, which stands 80m above the water and spans 170m.

5 PROSPECT POINT

Prospect Point, perched on a cliff, is the highest point in the park, where a cairn commemorates the SS *Beaver*, the pioneer steamship of the Pacific which sank near by in 1888.

6 SIWASH ROCK

Soon Siwash Rock juts defiantly skyward from the sea. Often a grey gull clings to the small tree on top of a tuft of green on the 15m-high column of grey rock. The rock is the subject of an Indian legend. Millennia ago a handsome young chief and his wife lived near by. As the chief plunged into the waters to cleanse himself to ensure a spotless life for their newborn son, a canoe containing four giants demanded that the chief go ashore. He refused, and they were so impressed by his devotion to the child, that they transformed him into Siwash Rock, to stand forever as a monument to Clean Fatherhood. The legend was recorded a century ago by Mohawk poet-princess Pauline Johnson, who is buried in a leafy glade near by. A stone monument marks her grave.

7 SECOND BEACH

Second Beach has a popular children's playground and a sandy beach, ideal for sunbathing and watching the sun set. On summer evenings, dancers take over the paved patio near by. The cycle trail crosses the main road through the park, and passes a Japanese-style bridge crossing a willow-banked stream. In the surrounding meadow, Canada geese graze for grain. Beyond are a pitch-and-putt golf course, lawn bowling, tennis courts and a fine Mediterranean-style restaurant. The trail continues over a humped bridge and follows the southern shore along Lost Lagoon to the start of the tour.

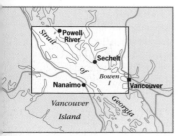

Sunshine Circle

Travellers trying to cram a lot into a two-week holiday in BC coastal country find a circle tour makes sense. This driving circuit includes four ferry rides (queues can be horrendous in summer) and covers the Sunshine Coast and eastern Vancouver Island. *Allow two to four days*

Begin at Horseshoe Bay, a 30-minute drive northwest from downtown Vancouver, where BC Ferries sail the 16km across Howe Sound to Langdale eight times a day.

1 GIBSONS

From Langdale, a 3km-long road winds west through forests and farmland along a craggy coastline to Gibsons, the gateway to the Sunshine Coast. Visitors like to tour Molly's Reach, the set where the television series, *The Beachcombers*, was filmed. Other options include a half-hour stroll along the sea walk to a stone cairn marking the spot where Captain Vancouver landed two centuries ago, poking into quaint shops along the main street, studying the Salish native displays and the 25,000 sea-

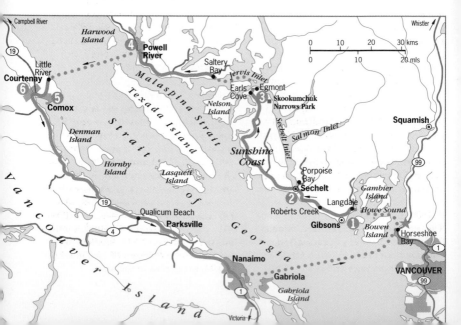

shells at the Elphinstone Pioneer Museum, and salmon fishing in nearby waters. West of Gibsons, just off the main road, are good beaches, hiking trails and picnic sites. Nearby Roberts Creek, a community of artists and artisans, has a camping site right on the water's edge.

2 SECHELT

About 14km northwest of Gibsons stands Sechelt, the commercial centre of the Sunshine Coast. Abundant and colourful marine life in the surrounding waters entertains scuba divers from near and far. Delicacies of the deep are served at the Wharf Restaurants on Davis Bay and the Blue Heron, where the large wading birds stalk shallow waters near by. The museum at the House of Héwhiwus ('house of chiefs') allows visitors to look back in time. The Sechelt natives, Canada's first self-governing aboriginal group, are renowned for fine carvings and woven cedar baskets.

3 SKOOKUMCHUK NARROWS

Beyond Sechelt, an hour's hike from Egmont leads to look-outs above the Skookumchuk Narrows, where strong tides (highest during the summer and winter solstices) from three inlets rush at speeds of up to 15 knots through the spectacular rock-strewn passage. A ferry connects nearby Earl's Cove with Saltery Bay across Jervis Inlet, where bald eagles fly overhead and playful killer whales, seals and sea lions compete for slow salmon. Divers can see the bronze mermaid anchored 20m down in Mermaid Cove.

4 POWELL RIVER

The next town, Powell River, is famous for fishing and the large pulp and paper mill which produced Western Canada's first roll of newsprint in 1912.

Ferries crossing Jervis Inlet

5 COMOX

Four ferries sail daily from Powell River to Comox on Vancouver Island, a 75-minute cruise west. Fishing, forestry, farming and tourism now sustain the Comox Valley, once known for coal mining. Reasonable property prices, a gentle pace and a moderate climate are attracting growing numbers of retired Canadians. Visitors come for the sandy beaches, the local handicrafts and the biennial air show. The historic Filbert Lodge and Park is a good place to enjoy afternoon tea followed by a stroll in the gardens.

6 COURTENAY

Another interesting place to walk is the adjacent town of Courtenay, where the downtown area has been remodelled with old-fashioned cobblestones and lamps and brick planters brimming with flowers. The Courtenay Museum and Archives boasts the largest log cabin in the world, built in 1928, where displays of fossils, dolls and Indian artefacts recall times past. *Allow about two hours for the winding road following the coast south to Nanaimo, and the ferry which takes two hours to sail back to Horseshoe Bay.*

What to See – Vancouver

*V*ancouver, commonly called the Gateway to the Pacific, is almost entirely surrounded by water. To the north is Burrard Inlet, an ice-free harbour where freighters fly flags from many nations. To the south, the Fraser River flows west into the Strait of Georgia, which separates Vancouver and the rest of the mainland from Vancouver Island. As a prairie farmer remarked, 'Vancouver would be great, if the view wasn't blocked by the mountains.' The sheltering ranges attract grey clouds that shower the city with 140cm of rain a year, resulting in fresh air and lush green landscapes. The clouds frost the peaks with snow for city skiing five months a year.

Metropolitan Vancouver covers 3,000sq km, including the suburbs of North Vancouver, West Vancouver, Burnaby, Coquitlam, Port Coquitlam, Port Moody, Pitt Meadows, Richmond, White Rock, Delta, and New Westminster, Surrey and Langley.

Although Vancouver is Canada's third largest centre (after Toronto and Montreal), the many waterways, mountains and parks lend the illusion of space.

While the past has been largely the story of seeking and selling natural resources, new industries are emerging. Skills now produce sightseeing submarines, satellite-sensing equipment, computer software and data terminal designs.

A growing tourism industry draws some visitors back as residents. Hotels continue to spring up in a city centre of skyscrapers. Well-developed facilities and roadways allow visitors and residents to ski in the morning, sail in the afternoon and enjoy opera in the evening. Even business seems a sport in this city, which has one of the most speculative stock markets in the world.

Most people come to Vancouver for the scenery, so first select one of its many vantage points for an overview of the city.

People who like to keep their feet firmly planted on the ground may prefer to stroll along the promenade deck at Canada Place, a good orientation spot. With its five white sails jutting out into the harbour, this city landmark features a dozen markers indicating sites of interest around the city.

You can also enjoy spectacular views from the air or from downtown city buildings.

AERIAL SIGHTSEEING
Harbour Air, BC's largest seaplane company, packages seven tours, varying from a half-hour flight over the city centre to a six-hour round-trip to Vancouver Island which includes stops at Victoria and Butchart Gardens. *Tel: 688-1277.*

Pegasus Ballooning Ltd offers the ultimate romantic adventure-aloft with the breeze over the verdant Fraser Valley, followed by a traditional champagne celebration upon landing. *Tel: 531-3400.*

Vancouver Helicopters offers scenic city and wilderness tours, departing from downtown and Grouse Mountain. Options range from a 20-minute flight over English Bay, Stanley Park and the Lions Gate Bridge to the two-hour Mountain Odyssey, which includes a 20-minute stopover on a glacier.
455 Commissioner Street. Tel: 683-HELI.

BIRD'S EYE VIEWPOINTS
Cloud Nine
The price of a meal or a drink at the Cloud Nine restaurant, atop the 42-storey Sheraton Landmark Hotel, includes a 360-degree view of Vancouver.
1400 Robson Street. Tel: 687-0511.

Harbour Centre
The glass elevators on the south side of Harbour Centre rise 167m to The Lookout! cafeteria, revolving restaurant and viewing deck, which features a 12-minute slide show about the city.
555 West Hastings Street. Tel: 689-0421.
Open: daily 9am-10pm. Admission charge.

Vistas on the Bay
Gourmets of both food and scenery love the revolving Vistas restaurant at the top of the Ramada Renaissance Hotel.
1133 West Hastings Street. Tel: 689-9211.
Viewing free.

Seen from the air, downtown Vancouver nudges Stanley Park into Burrard Inlet

Beaches

Sunset volleyball at
Kitsilano Beach

Sunworshippers
Kitsila

Picnicking at
Locarno Beach

Windsurfing
on English Bay

Lovers of BC's wild rainforest say nothing compares with a wintry day walk along a misty, deserted beach with waterproof boots, a broad umbrella and a frisky dog.

On New Year's Day in Vancouver, however, around 2,000 locals dash into English Bay for the Polar Bear Swim. No one lingers long; they dress quickly and head indoors to recuperate from the chilling waters.

But summer is another story. Beaches become crowded with swimmers, sand-castle builders, frisbee players, windsurfers, kite flyers and sunseekers who want to do exactly nothing. An occasional canine slips in without permission, and squirrels sometimes appear hoping for handouts. Especially towards sunset, an entrepreneur with a metal detector in hand may sift the sands hoping for hidden treasures.

Although many people bring picnics, alcohol is not allowed; but it is rumoured that every now and then a thermos brings in wine masquerading as Kool-Aid.

There are sandy shores, gravel shores and pebble shores. English Bay's Sunset Beach is ribboned with gigantic trunks from rainforest trees that have escaped from log booms, a reminder that timber is an important industry here. The logs are great for leaning on, and they provide some privacy. Some are big enough for a single sunbather to stretch right out on top.

Although the sun is tempered by refreshing offshore breezes, it's wise to wear a strong sunscreen for protection against the direct rays and those reflected off the sea and sand.

West Vancouver's Ambleside Beach is one of the few city beaches to permit campfires. It's wonderful to roast hot dogs and marshmallows around a flickering fire as the Lions Gate Bridge lights up and the sailboats and freighters and the sunset fade into the darkening evening sky over English Bay.

Flying kites on a beach near Nanaimo on Vancouver Island

Beaches

*A*lthough beachcombing is a pleasant pastime come rain or shine in winter, Vancouver beaches are at their best in summer. From Victoria Day to Labour Day, lifeguards supervise the city's 10 swimming beaches from 11.30am to 9pm. There is no admission charge to the beaches, and changing rooms, toilets and refreshment stands are found in many convenient locations.

Kitsilano Beach is a popular venue for spending a day lazing in the warm sun

ENGLISH BAY
Fifteen minutes from downtown Vancouver, English Bay sports several fine beaches.

Kitsilano Beach
Kitsilano Beach has a heated outdoor saltwater pool overlooking that great unheated pool, English Bay. Nearby Jericho Beach, Locarno Beach and Spanish Banks are favourites with windsurfers. There is adequate parking, and food stalls and picnic tables are scattered along the beach.
Southwest of the Burrard Street Bridge.

Second Beach
This beach features a tidal saltwater pool which protects children from the currents, and there are areas for picnics and barbecues and for playing soccer, football, volleyball and baseball.
In Stanley Park, north of Sunset Beach.

Sunset Beach
At this beach, the closest to downtown, summer sunsets are glorious. Residents and visitors congregate on giant logs on the beach or sip sundowners at the front tables in the nearby English Bay Café and the Sylvia Hotel to contemplate the end of another day.
At the corner of Pacific Avenue and Jervis Street.

Third Beach
This isolated beach is relatively quiet.
On the west side of Stanley Park, north of Second Beach and Ferguson Point.

Wreck Beach
This beach has unrivalled natural beauty. A steep trail (not easy to find, ask directions) winds down to the water from North West Marine Drive to this unspoiled wild strand, the only one in the Lower Mainland.
On the tip of the Point Grey peninsula near the University of British Columbia (UBC).

Chinatown

*V*ancouver's thriving Chinatown, a 10-minute walk from the city centre, stretches over six blocks, north to south from Main Street to the Georgia Street viaduct and east to west from Gore Street to Carrall Street. Millions of dollars change hands here every day, in more than a dozen banks and hundreds of businesses ranging from food to electronics. Chinese immigrants bring in an estimated $2 billion to BC every year.

Chinatown is home to a few thousand permanent residents, mostly elderly. Most Chinese Canadians live in other parts of the city, but many come to Chinatown to bank, shop and eat. As a result, the streets bustle with activity. Shops overflowing with rosewood furniture, bamboo and wickerware, jade jewellery and porcelain stand cheek-by-jowl with herbal pharmacies and Cantonese, Mandarin and Szechwan restaurants, most of which serve excellent food at reasonable prices.

A pot-pourri of colourful shops awaits visitors to Vancouver's busy Chinatown

CHINESE CULTURAL CENTRE
Situated between Carrall and Columbia streets (see page 24) the Chinese Cultural Centre houses changing exhibitions of traditional culture and local history and sponsors the annual Chinese New Year Parade.
50 East Pender Street. Tel: 687–0729. Open: daily 10am–60m. Admission free.

DR SUN YAT-SEN CHINESE GARDEN
This garden (see page 24), opened for Expo 86, was created in classical Chinese style and is a harmonious blend of plants and space, with numerous terraces, pavilions and walkways.
578 Carrall Street. Tel: 662–3207. Open: daily 10am–4.30pm in winter. Admission charge.

SAM KEE BUILDING
This two-storey structure, the narrowest building in the world, was built in 1913. Measuring 1.8m by 30m, it was once the home of a Chinese family and now houses an insurance company (see page 26).
At the southwest corner of Pender and Carrall Street. Not open to the public, but can be viewed from outside.

Churches

*T*here are dozens of places of worship in Vancouver, of every faith and denomination, thanks to the variety of visitors from all over the world who eventually settled here and brought their religious beliefs and practices with them. A listing of churches is found in the Practical Guide section on pages 185–6, but following are a few that might be of interest to anyone, regardless of creed.

BUDDHIST TEMPLE

This temple is an exquisite example of Chinese palatial architecture, with gilded porcelain tiles and flying rooftop dragons. The interior is an artistic showcase of oriental sculpture, painting, carpentry and embroidery. An outdoor courtyard encloses a beautiful collection of bonsai plants and a ceramic mural of Kuan-Yin-Bodhisattva.

A 30-minute drive south from downtown; turn west at the exit by Fantasy Gardens towards Steveston. 9160 Steveston Highway, Richmond. Tel: 274–2822. Open: daily 10am–5pm. Free.

CANADIAN MEMORIAL CHURCH

Shortly after World War I, Chaplain George Fallis came to Vancouver with the idea of building a memorial to Canadians who had served in the war. He found a congregation with the same idea, solicited the support of local leaders, and then headed east across Canada to find further funding. The result was the Canadian Memorial Church, which opened in 1928 at the 11th hour of the 11th day of the 11th month – mortgage-free.

Although the church is constructed in attractive greystone gothic-style, the stained-glass windows are the main attraction. Each window depicts a Biblical scene, with the provincial coat of arms beneath flanked by illustrations of historical events.

The BC window depicts a soldier's faith, with Christ meeting a Roman centurion pleading on behalf of his palsied servant. The historic panels show Captain Vancouver at Nootka Sound in 1792 and Simon Fraser exploring the Fraser River in 1808.

The Nova Scotia window illustrates the arrival of Jacques Cartier in 1543 and of Lord Rollo, the first Englishman, in 1759. The Yukon window depicts the Chilkoot Pass in 1898 and a Royal Mail dog team with cariole.

The spectacular chancel window portrays a biblical motif of sacrifice and young manhood. The all-Canada window facing north depicts the services rendered by all men and women of Canada throughout World War I.

The windows are interesting for their comments on world peace and history and for their exquisite craftsmanship.

At the southwest corner of Burrard Street and Fifteenth Avenue. Tel: 731–3101. Open: regular church services are held Sunday morning at 10.30 hrs, but for many visitors who may prefer to study the windows in relative solitude, staff at the community centre, adjacent to the church on Sixteenth Avenue, keep the keys and escort those interested to the chapel during regular business hours.

CHRIST CHURCH CATHEDRAL

Located in the heart of downtown Vancouver, this century-old sanctuary looks as though it should be nestled into a green valley in rural England. Of special interest are the English and Canadian stained-glass windows and a tableau of the *Crucifixion*.
690 Burrard Street. Tel: 682-3848. Open: daily 10am–4pm. Free.

WESTMINSTER ABBEY

This modern Benedictine monastery is both a high school and a degree-granting theological seminary. Every Sunday the 10 bells of the 50m tower chime over the valley to announce mass. Resident

A haven of tranquillity: the courtyard of the Buddhist Temple in Richmond

monks create and restore paintings and other art forms in an atmosphere of peace and tranquillity. Various sculptures, stained-glass windows and murals decorate the monastery. Overnight rooms are available (reservations recommended), as St Benedict believed that there should always be guests at a monastery.
Located near the town of Mission, an hour's drive east from Vancouver. Tel: 826–8975. Open: daily 2pm–4pm. Guided tours available; modest dress requested. Donations accepted.

Festivals and Special Events

*V*ancouver has numerous special events scheduled all year round, but the majority of these take place in summer. Visitors are welcome to participate.

January
Every New Year's Day, more than 2,000 Vancouverites and visitors plunge into the chilly winter waters of English Bay for the **Polar Bay Swim**.

The Chinese New Year Dragon Parade – two weeks of colourful displays

February
The Chinese New Year celebrations are highlighted by the Dragon Parade along Pender Street in Chinatown, where colourful dragons dance to the sound of drums and eat money offered by local merchants to ensure prosperity.

April
The **Hyack Festival** in New Westminster features an Easter Parade of antique cars.

May
The **Cloverdale Rodeo**, held at the fairgrounds, is one of the largest rodeos on the continent. The **Vancouver Children's Festival**, held in red candy-stripe tents in Vanier Park, presents crafts, acrobats, theatre, mime, puppetry, music and dance from around the world. May is also **Rhododendron Month** at the VanDusen Gardens.

June
At the 10-day **International du Maurier Jazz Festival**, artists from all over the world play jazz and blues at the Plaza of Nations, several shopping malls and more intimate spots throughout the city.

The Plaza of Nations and Pacific Place are the sites of the **Dragon Boat Festival**, where competitors from all over the world paddle their hearts out. Food, fireworks, and street theatre and music accompany the colourful parade of sleek oriental craft gliding along False Creek. The **Gastown Grand Prix Bicycle Race** over cobblestone streets is an exciting spectacle.

July
Canada Day, which marks the nation's birthday on 1 July, is celebrated with picnics and parades and evening fireworks. **Vancouver Sea Festival**, which focuses on the Sunset Beach area, is the biggest local festival of the year. A week of maritime events includes a heritage boat show, a sailing regatta, an international food fair, a chocolate mermaid treasure hunt and a raft of entertainers, all capped by spectacular fireworks and the **Nanaimo**

to **English Bay Bathtub Race,** a
bizarre display of bravado and technical
skill.

Musicians from around the world
perform at the **Folk Music Festival** at
Jericho Beach Park. In the **Work Boat
Parade,** which ends at the quay in New
Westminster, the tugboat ballet delights
the hearts of young and old.

August

Abbotsford Airport (an hour's drive east
from Vancouver) is the site of the three-
day **Abbotsford Air Show,** featuring
aerial acrobatics by the Canadian
Snowbirds, the Blue Angels from
California, skydivers and wing-walkers,
along with an exhibition of antique and
experimental aircraft.

At the **Pacific National Exhibition**
at Exhibition Park in East Vancouver,
there are livestock displays, equestrian
events, dog shows, log rolling and
bungy jumping, and the downtown
parade.

Children love the fun at Playland
and the Kids' World play centre. The
Teddy Bear Fair at Deas Island
Regional Park, Delta, is also popular
with youngsters. The **Powell Street
Festival,** dedicated to the history, arts
and culture of Asian Canadians, is a
mosaic of colourful costumes, sumo
wrestling, food and music from all
over the Orient.

September

Particularly popular are the innovative
performances at the **Vancouver Fringe
Festival** held at various theatres in or
near downtown, and the **Aldergrove
Fall Fair,** primarily an agricultural
harvest fair.

October

Thanksgiving celebrations take place at
the Burnaby Village Museum and the
International Writers' Festival on

*The unmistakable artistic style of the East
at a Vancouver Japanese festival*

Granville Island. **Octoberfest
Weekends** at the Commodore Ballroom
are a hit with the young and lively.

December

Carol Cruises around English Bay
brighten the short dark days of winter,
with a parade of lights and Christmas
carolers. **First Night** on New Year's Eve
has become a popular way to end the old
and begin the new. Thousands of people
wander around the city enjoying indoor
and outdoor entertainers.

Timeless
sculpture by
Canada's First
Nations
embellishes
the English
Bay shore

Exhibits in the
Inuit Gallery,
Gastown

Art on displ
Kitsilano B

The unusual exterior
of the Eagle Aerie
Gallery, Tofino

A fine example of Inuit art

The BC Art Scene

Nature has been and continues to be an inspiration and the dominating influence motivating local artists. It is clearly evident in their work, from the powerful and mysterious moods of old-growth rain forests and totem poles painted by Emily Carr to the subtle watercolour seascapes of contemporary Toni Onley.

Emily Carr, born in Victoria in 1871, is acknowledged as the grand matriarch of BC art. Her inspiration came from both the natural surroundings and the original inhabitants, as she travelled the BC coast collecting and portraying a wealth of impressions from First Nations peoples, their arts and their legends.

Other BC greats include such masters as Bill Reid, Reg Davidson and Roy Vickers, who all have a native heritage; European immigrants John Coerner from Czechoslovakia and Bratsa Bonisacho from Yugoslavia; Attila Rick Lukacs, originally from Alberta; and such developing talents as John Penhall and Lorraine Yabuki.

Since the 1980s, local artists have artistically expressed a strong commentary on preserving the environment and on controversies centring around fishing, logging and endangered species.

Local photographers Jeff Wall, Rodney Graham, Fred Douglas and Marion Penner-Bancroft have earned international renown. And sculptors Roland Brennen and Mowry Baden, using plastics, electronics and other 20th-century products, have set a new direction for west coast sculpture with their kinetic creations.

In addition to the contemporary works of resident painters, sculptors and photographers, local galleries exhibit First Nations cedar carvings and paintings, with their traditional colourful oval designs; Inuit soapstone sculptures from the Arctic; works by the Canadian Group of Seven; and old European and Asian masters.

Galleries

*V*ancouver is a young city, and youthful energy and enthusiasm is reflected in the freshness of its art scene, both in traditional West Coast art and in the more avant-garde work. Since galleries often close to mount new shows and because some are staffed by volunteers, it is often wise to phone ahead.

DOWNTOWN

The **Alexander Gallery**, at 1249 Howe Street (tel: 681–8848), houses a fine collection of contemporary work; go upstairs to see a unique private collection.

A Walk Is, at 976 Denman Street (tel: 682–0060), features fresh and vivid work by young contemporary artists.

Buschlen-Mowatt, 1445 West Georgia Street (tel: 682–1234), stages dramatic international quality shows, with ongoing emphasis on Miró and Picasso.

Catriona Jeffries, in an office building at 550 Burrard Street (tel: 683–2415), exhibits interesting contemporary local art.

The **Marion Scott Gallery**, at 671 Howe Street (tel: 685–1934), features Inuit, aboriginal and Northwest Coast native art.

The **Sergio Bustamente Gallery**, at 1130 Mainland Street (tel: 684–1340) displays the whimsical work of this renowned Mexican artist.

The **Vancouver Art Gallery**, at 750 Hornby Street (tel: 682–5621), once home to the provincial law courts, is a neoclassical heritage building and a work of art itself. It houses paintings by early 20th-century Canadian artists known as the Group of Seven; evocative rainforest works by Emily Carr (1871–1945); works by Dutch, Italian, French, German and English masters; and photography, sculpture, graphics and video works.

You can wander around on your own or join a free 20-minute tour. The reference-only library, gift shop and restaurant make the Vancouver Art Gallery a rainy-day special.

GASTOWN

The **Crown Gallery**, at 562 Beatty Street (tel: 684–5407), displays contemporary Canadian art.

The **Exposures Gallery**, at 851 Beatty Street (tel: 688–6853), features photography.

The **Inuit Gallery**, at 345 Water Street (tel: 688–7323), exhibits and sells excellent traditional Inuit masterworks, Cape Dorset Inuit sculpture, and West Coast native Indian works.

The **Perel Gallery**, at 112 West Hastings (tel: 681–5820), is run by up-and-coming young art students from Simon Fraser University. Call for an appointment. The **SFU Art Gallery** in Harbour Centre (tel: 291–4266) is also worth a visit.

The **Smash Gallery of Modern Art**, at 160 West Cordova Street (tel: 662–7200), features aggressive contemporary art.

The **Video Inn**, at 1102 Homer Street (tel: 688–4336), houses a collection of contemporary Western

Canadian video works.

Women in Focus, at 857 Beatty Street (tel: 682–5848), displays contemporary art by Canadian women.

GRANVILLE ISLAND

The **Charles H Scott Gallery** in the Emily Carr College of Art and Design, at 1399 Johnston Street, Granville Island (tel: 844–3809), mounts travelling shows. You can also walk through the school and look at students' work.

Leona Lattimer, at 1590 West 2nd (tel: 732–4556), sells many current works by First Nation artists.

SOUTH GRANVILLE

The **Alexander Harrison Galleries**, at 2932 Granville Street (tel: 732–5217), specialise in Canadian turn-of-the-century art.

The **Atelier Gallery**, at 3084 Granville Street (tel: 732–3021), sells contemporary art.

Bau-Xi Gallery, at 3045 Granville Street (tel: 733–7011), features international-standard contemporary art. Be sure to look upstairs as well.

The **George Cromartie Gallery**, at 2818 Granville Street (tel: 736–6625), runs a small art centre for seminars and art shows, and has a permanent Stephen Denslow collection.

Diane Farris, at 1565 West 7th Avenue (tel: 737–2629), is the place to watch the careers of such young romantics as Richard Lukacs and Angela Grossman.

The **Dorian Rae Collection**, 3151 Granville Street (tel: 732–6100), is a long-time importer of Asian and African art and artefacts.

Equinox Gallery, at 2321 Granville Street (tel: 736–2405), features international 20th-century shows.

The **Gallery of Tribal Art** is located at 1521 West 8th Avenue (tel: 732–4555).

Petley Jones, at 2245 Granville Street (tel: 732–5353), features contemporary and older works in dealer's stock.

OTHER GALLERIES

The **Western Front**, at 303 East 8th Avenue (tel: 876–9343), is the premier parallel gallery in Canada, with artist-managed gallery space.

The **Alex Fraser**, at 2027 West 41st Avenue (tel: 266–6010), has an excellent *fin-de-siècle* collection, especially of Quebec artists.

The impressive Vancouver Art Gallery, with its excellent Emily Carr collection, has fine displays of international art

Gardens and Parks

*E*very February, when most of Canada is still covered in ice and snow, the first crocuses of spring poke their heads above ground to take a look at Vancouver and Victoria. The temperate coastal climate, ample sunshine and abundant rainfall encourage and ensure a great diversity of colourful flora. The greenery, which reigns supreme most of the year, is upstaged by riots of colourful blossom in spring and summer.

There are more than 150 gardens and parks in Vancouver, not counting the hundreds of thousands of private yards and gardens. Two of the prettiest public oases in the city differ greatly in character. Wild and rambling Stanley Park (see pages 40–1 and 76–9), is western, while the Dr Sun Yat-sen Chinese Garden (see page 24) is typically eastern.

BOTANICAL GARDENS AT THE UNIVERSITY OF BRITISH COLUMBIA

This showcase of plants from around the world includes a physic garden for medicinal herbs, planted around a sundial in the geometric design of a 16th-century herb garden. Horticulturists here have developed such new plants as the Emerald Carpet, a practical, low-spreading ground-cover plant with little flowers. The Arbour Garden provides cool shade where vines abound year round, while the Food Garden grows fruit trees trained in traditional styles, and the latest vegetables. The Asian Garden features 300 species of rhododendrons along with kiwi fruit vines, magnolias and rhododendrons.

SW Marine Drive. Tel: 822–3928. Open: daily 10am–dusk. Admission charge.

NITOBE MEMORIAL GARDEN

Reflecting the private retreats of Japan, gentle walkways meander through artistically pruned cherry, maple and pine trees, and layouts of sand and rock, to a tiny teahouse. The cherry blossoms in April or May and the iris blooms in late June are spectacular.

Across the street from the UBC Botanical Gardens. Tel: 822–3928. Open: daily 10am–dusk. Admission charge.

PARK AND TILFORD GARDENS

This privately owned hide-away offers a delightful variety of plantings and landscape themes.

333 Brooksbank Avenue, North Vancouver. Tel: 984–8200. Open: daily dawn–dusk.

QUEEN ELIZABETH PARK

This 52-hectare former stone quarry, transformed into sunken gardens, is a favourite site for bridal couples and wedding photos amid lawns, trees, shrubs and flowers. It is the highest spot in the city (152m), so views are spectacular. The blossoms are at their best in late May and June, when azaleas and rhododendrons create a brilliant kaleidoscope of colour. An arboretum on the east side showcases trees and shrubs indigenous to the BC coast.

There is also a rose garden, a pitch-

The spectacular colours of autumn foliage in Queen Elizabeth Park

and-putt golf course, 20 tennis courts and a restaurant looking out to the city. The Bloedel Floral Conservatory, a 20m-high triodetic dome consisting of 1,490 plexiglass bubbles, houses a tropical garden with more than 100 colourful birds flying free, and an arid area with cacti and seasonal floral displays.

*33rd Avenue at Cambie Street.
Tel: 872– 5513. Open: daily 10am–9pm in summer, 10am–5pm October to mid–April. Admission charge to the conservatory.*

VANDUSEN BOTANICAL GARDEN
Once a golf course, this 22-hectare site now displays ornamental grasses, glorious clusters of rhodo-dendrons and heathers and an encyclopaedic collection of West Coast conifers. The Sino-Himalayan Garden, sometimes called 'the mother of gardens', is a tribute to China. Other attractions include an Elizabethan-style walk-through maze, a topiary garden for children, guided tours, a gift shop with a floral theme and Sprinklers Restaurant.

37th and Oak Streets, not far from Queen Elizabeth Park. Tel: 266–7194. Open: daily 10am–dusk. Admission charge.

Vancouver Harbour

*V*ancouver, Canada's largest port and one of the top 20 in the world, is the country's gateway to the Pacific Rim and plays an exciting role in international trade. Every year more than 3,000 ships, most flying foreign flags, carry bulk, general and containerised cargo between Vancouver and a hundred other ports around the world. The two dozen terminals circling Vancouver Harbour move more than 70 million tonnes of cargo annually. Enterprises engaged in this trade range from BC Sugar and United Grain Growers to Cassier Mining and the Saskatchewan Wheat Pool.

Beyond the Inner Harbour east of Second Narrows Bridge are several oil refineries and a major sulphur export operation at Port Moody. About 35km south of downtown, near the BC Ferries dock at Tsawwassen, the Westshore Terminals at Roberts Bank ship coal, sulphur and lumber to other countries.

A Behind-the-Scenes Look
Vanterm, at the north foot of Clark Drive, has an observation deck for viewing a major container terminal, along with a theatre where an informative audio-visual show explains port operations. The viewing area is open year round from Tuesday to Friday

Pleasure craft and houseboats line the waterfront at Vancouver's Coal Harbour

for self-directed tours. Guided tours are offered from June to August on Sunday afternoons.

Canada Place Promenade

Canada Place has a wrap-around public promenade for observing the Inner Harbour. A self-directed walk, called 'Promenade Into History', follows a series of plaques describing historical waterfront events. The promenade also provides great dockside viewing of some of the world's most luxurious cruise ships, which run from here to Alaska from May to September.

Panoramic Vantage Points

Harbour-view rooms at the Pan Pacific, Waterfront Centre and Ramada Renaissance hotels enable visitors to Vancouver to get orientated quickly. Much cheaper are the bird's-eye vantage points at Vistas, the revolving restaurant atop the Ramada Renaissance Hotel, where visitors can enjoy regional specialities or coffee and dessert as the harbour panorama moves by. The Lookout!, a circular observation deck high above Harbour Centre, also affords a 360-degree view of the harbour and the city, and photographic plaques and decorative display panels relate the history and character of the area. But there is an admission charge.

Views from the Water

For a view of the harbour from the water, take the SeaBus from the downtown terminal to North Vancouver. Alternatively, contact any Travel Info-Centre for details about harbour cruises.

Waterfront Parks

Several parks around Burrard Inlet offer

The North Shore across Burrard Inlet

great picnic spots and harbour views. From the Stanley Park Port Look Out, on the seawall just south of Brockton Point, almost the whole harbour is visible and a series of plaques outlines port operations.

Much smaller Portside Park, just east of Canada Place at the foot of Main Street, offers grassy slopes, children's play areas and a good view of various marine activities. New Brighton Park, further east and adjacent to the Alberta Wheat Pool just off McGill Street, has a pool, a pier and lots of open space. From here there are views of the facilities handling grain and forest products and of ships sailing through the Second Narrows.

Waterfront Park, located between the Lonsdale Quay and the Pacific Marine Training Institute in North Vancouver, provides a panorama of the harbour and the city skyline. Harbour View Park, located further east on a narrow strip of land at the mouth of Lynn Creek, features a creekside walking trail and a platform for observing the loading and unloading of forest products.

Harbour Life

Vancouver Harbour, once almost exclusively industrial, is becoming more liveable all the time. Plans are underway for drastic redevelopment along Coal Harbour between the Bayshore and Pan Pacific hotels, which will create a variety of town homes and apartments for waterfront living just 10-minutes' walk from downtown. The proposed residential marina will have complete waste-disposal

Boat moorings at Coal Harbour

North Shore peaks and Burrard Inlet from Coal Harbour

facilities, and should also improve air quality, since more Vancouverites will be able to walk to work. About 60 per cent of West Enders already walk or cycle downtown to work. Half of the 16-hectare Coal Harbour development will be devoted to parks and open space, and Harbour Green waterfront park will be one of the largest downtown parks.

The pace of life in that part of the harbour occupied by pleasure craft is gentle. Residents here usually find time to chat and are friendly to visitors. One resident, who has worked here aboard his floating electronic cottage/house-boat for 18 years, says the tides are for him the pulse of Mother Nature. He travels 5km a year without leaving home, since harbour tides advance and retreat as much as 4.5m twice daily. Canada geese paddle up to his houseboat most mornings for breakfast, while hunched blue herons stalk along the shore for snacks, and kingfishers dive for minnows. Loons and cormorants patrol the waters, along with ever-present shrieking seagulls. Starfish and mussels hug the pillars that keep the docks in place, while crabs crawl and feed along the bottom. Harbour seals occasion-ally watch from further offshore.

In winter, harbour dwellers can pull out binoculars and look up to Grouse Mountain across Burrard Inlet to see if there's still room for more skiers on the slopes. It's quite a lifestyle!

A backdrop of skyscrapers at Coal Harbour

Floating homes in False Creek on Granville Island

Historic Houses

*V*ancouver, like Los Angeles, seems to have suffered from the philosophy of down with the old and up with the new, as far as preserving historic ('heritage') homes is concerned. But a few treasures remain.

Once a luxurious private home, historic Hy's Mansion now contains a restaurant

HY'S MANSION

This elegant Victorian stone mansion was built in 1900 by American sugar tycoon B T Rogers as a family residence. The original home had 18 fireplaces with self-cleaning flues (several of which remain) and a pantry cooled by ice. The walls are oak-panelled, and the floors are laid with teak from Fiji. A spectacular stained-glass window overlooks the staircase which rises from the main foyer. It depicts three women believed to represent the virtues of faith, hope and charity and the graces of wisdom, youth and beauty. The background is decorated with BC wildflowers and seashells.

Other features of the house include a walk-in humidor for cigar-smokers and, outside, a wrought-iron fence built from balconies of the old San Francisco city hall. It now houses a restaurant, noted for its excellent steaks, and is open evenings only.

1523 Davie Street, a five-minute walk from English Bay. Tel: 689–1111.

IRVING HOUSE

'The handsomest, the best and most home-like house of which BC can yet boast' was the 1865 newspaper description of this 14-room home, which originally belonged to 'King of the River' Captain William Irving. The small parlour and master bedroom contain Irving's furniture, including a red rocking chair from a Fraser River sternwheeler, a piano shipped round Cape Horn in 1858 and a black horsehair settee transported across the plains from Missouri. The kitchen features a classic black and chrome pioneer stove laden with cast-iron pots and flat irons, and a hand-pumped vacuum cleaner. The kitchen floor was laid and caulked like the deck of a ship. The nursery upstairs contains a collection of dolls from the 19th century. In the library are a roll-top desk, a smoking table, a pump organ, a 17th-century grandfather clock and a ladder to reach the upper shelves of books.
302 Royal Avenue, New Westminster. Tel: 521–7656. Open: Tuesday to Sunday 11am–5pm, May to mid-September; Saturday and Sunday 1pm–5pm in winter. Admission by donation.

ROEDDE HOUSE

Built in 1893 by the German immigrant Gustav Roedde, Vancouver's first bookbinder, this house is part of a park site that includes nine Victorian West End houses, most of them renovated for family accommodation.

Designed by F M Rattenbury, the architect responsible for the Empress Hotel, Roedde House is built in simple Queen Anne style, with a cupola, bay windows, an upstairs porch and a downstairs verandah. The interior has been furnished with period furniture to reflect city life at the turn of the century.
1415 Barclay Street, a 10-minute walk from the city centre. Tel: 684–7040. Open: Sunday 2pm–4pm and by appointment. Admission by donation.

The rich furnishings of Irving House are elegant reminders of times gone by

LE GAVROCHE

A good way to make the past present is by enjoying a meal in a heritage home restaurant. Named for the street urchin in *Les Misérables*, Le Gavroche is located in a refurbished three-storey Victorian house whose roof is green with moss, looking out to the Bayshore Hotel and Coal Harbour. The intimate dimly-lit interior, with its oak floors, flickering flames in the wood-burning fireplace, and dark floral print wallpaper contrasting with white tablecloths, quickly transports diners back to a more romantic time. The restaurant is renowned for refined service, fine French cuisine and one of the city's best wine collections.
1616 Alberni Street. Tel: 685–3924.

Museums

A wide variety of city museums provide an in-depth look at the history and cultural life of Vancouver and BC, with exhibits ranging from food and maritime history to sports and First Nations cultures.

MUSEUM OF ANTHROPOLOGY

The Museum of Anthropology at the University of British Columbia, probably Canada's most memorable museum, is best known for its superb collection of art and artefacts of the province's First Nations peoples. The spectacular concrete and glass structure sits on a cliff overlooking English Bay and, beyond, the North Shore Mountains and Howe Sound. Inside the MOA, as it is affectionately called, a dozen galleries house a great variety of objects, which express the complex social and ceremonial life of many cultures from around the world.

Entrance to the world of art

The museum's cedar entrance doors, designed and carved by contemporary 'Ksan master carvers, depict the joining of heaven and earth in the creation of the first Gitksan people. The doors, along with the adjoining side panels, form a rectangular structure inspired by the traditional Indian bent box. Carvings from traditional West Coast house interiors, with illustrations showing their original placement, border the entrance ramp. At the base of the ramp, a bear sculpted by the contemporary artist Bill Reid, of the Haida people, is one of the few touchable exhibits in the museum. Be sure to feel its square snout and large teeth, nostrils and ears, characteristic of the Haida bears.

The spectacular Great Hall

In the Great Hall, natural light streams through 14m-high windows, which illuminate an exquisite assembly of weathered cedar totem poles. Totem poles do not usually tell a story, but depict creatures representing the genealogy of the families that raised them. Ravens, bears, beavers, frogs, eagles and wolves are often an integral part of tribal crests. Totem poles have traditionally been raised to identify families or to commemorate the departed, and a raising continues to be an occasion for a potlatch, or celebration. A selection of red cedar chests and carved canoes and dishes complements the elegant totem poles displayed here.

Highlights of the galleries

The Masterpiece Gallery houses an intriguing collection of intricately carved miniatures in silver, gold, argillite, ivory, bone, horn and wood, mostly dating from the 19th century.

But the highlight of the contemporary collection is the acclaimed sculpture *Raven and the First Men*, carved in laminated yellow cedar by Bill Reid, and displayed in a skylighted rotunda. The sculpture is a dramatic portrayal of the birth of mankind, with the first Haida people emerging both frontwards and backwards from a partially open clam shell.

On the UBC campus at 6393 Marine Drive. Tel: 822–3825. Open: daily 11am–5pm, extended Tuesday to 9pm. Closed: Monday from September to June, also 25 and 26 December. Admission charge, except Tuesday.

The Theatre Gallery displays a permanent collection of fine examples of First Nations masks, along with changing temporary exhibits.

Gallery Nine houses a permanent exhibition of more than 4,000 colourful textiles and articles of clothing from around the world.

The Research Collections Room, since the museum is both a public and a teaching institution, features a visible storage system, with a series of glass-covered drawers that let visitors see but not touch more than 10,000 objects,

In the Museum of Anthropology is a fine collection of Northwest Coast Indian art

arranged in cultural and artefact categories.

The outdoor exhibits

One of the best exhibits is outdoors on the grassy area between the museum and the cliff. The Kwakiutl and Gitksan totem poles standing here with two Haida houses, one for the living and one for the dead, are completely at one with nature.

Museums

ABLE WALKER MUSEUM

This transportation exhibit depicts the settlement of North America, probably the largest movement of people and materials the world has ever known. *2350 Beta Avenue, Burnaby. Tel: 299–3444. Open: Monday to Friday 9am–4.30pm.*

BC SPORTS HALL OF FAME AND MUSEUM

This museum provides high-tech, hands-on sports entertainment. Visitors can run, swim, hop and slide their way through the computer-enhanced Hall of Champions which honours BC's elite athletes and teams, or test their athletic

The H R MacMillan Planetarium provides exciting glimpses of the universe

skills against top competitors in the Participation Gallery. The museum covers 150 years of history, from an 1860s Victorian picnic to a recently televised pro game. Real-life athletes and teams give demonstrations of their skills. *At BC Place Stadium. Tel: 687–5520. Open: daily 10am–5pm.*

CANADIAN CRAFT MUSEUM

Located in the courtyard behind Cathedral Place, this newcomer on the local scene houses a fascinating collection of *objets d'art* crafted from

clay, wood, glass, metal and fibre. Special features are the glass door and window created by renowned stained-glass artist Lutz Haufschild.
639 Hornby Street. Tel: 687–8266. Open: Monday to Saturday 9.30am–5.30pm, Sundays and holidays noon–5pm. Admission charge.

H R MACMILLAN PLANETARIUM

This educational centre, considered one of North America's finest, offers journeys through time and space with entertaining and informative programmes including astronomy laser shows.
1100 Chestnut Street in Vanier Park. Tel: 736–3656. Open: Tuesday to Sunday, with shows at 2pm and 5.30pm; additional shows at 1pm and 4pm on weekends and holidays. Admission charge.

At the nearby Gordon Southam Observatory, visitors can gaze through a large telescope at the distant worlds of the sun, moon, stars, comets, planets and galaxies.
Open: Tuesday to Sunday noon–5pm and 7pm–11pm; reservations advised.

VANCOUVER MARITIME MUSEUM

Identified by the tall Kwakiutl totem pole which stands in front, this museum highlights the history of marine exploration, sailing, fishing, maritime art and the developments of the port of Vancouver. Adjacent Heritage Harbour is now home to the *St Roch*, a two-masted schooner which is now a National Historic Site. Built in the 1920s, it became the first ship to navigate through the treacherous waters of the Northwest Passage from west to east.
1905 Ogden Avenue. Tel: 737–2212. Open: daily 10am–5pm. Closed Christmas Day. Tours every 30 minutes. Admission charge.

CAPTAIN GEORGE VANCOUVER

About two centuries ago, George Vancouver, an English youth of Dutch descent, joined the British navy at age 13. He eventually served with Captain Cook on his second and third voyages.

In 1791, Captain Vancouver set out from England aboard the HMS *Discovery*, sailed south around the Cape of Good Hope, and a year later reached the northern Pacific coast of North America. He had been commissioned to survey the coast and negotiate a land settlement with Spanish Captain Bodega y Quadra, at Nootka, on what is now known as Vancouver Island.

Without realising that the Spaniards had charted this region before him, Vancouver claimed all the land he saw for King George III.

Vancouver returned to England in 1795 and died three years later aged 40. Spain eventually became sidetracked by the Mexican revolution and abandoned all claims to the Pacific Northwest.

VANCOUVER MUSEUM

This museum, which houses one of the largest civic collections in Canada, is devoted to regional history and the First Nations, but also features exhibitions of decorative arts from Asia, Europe and the Americas.
1100 Chestnut Street. Tel: 736–4431. Open: daily 10am–5pm; hours extended Monday to Friday to 9pm in summer. Closed: Mondays September to May and Christmas Day. Admission charge.

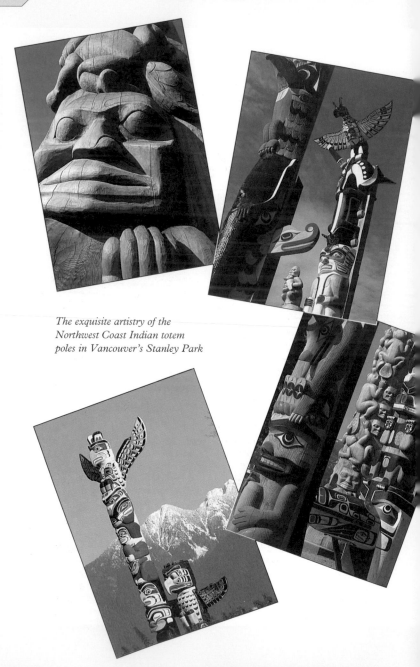

The exquisite artistry of the Northwest Coast Indian totem poles in Vancouver's Stanley Park

On the Totem Trail

At least 8,000 years ago, Asian peoples who lived by hunting and gathering berries crossed the icy land bridge that is now the Bering Strait and drifted south along the Pacific coast of North America and into the interior. When the Europeans arrived in the late 18th century, an estimated 80,000 of these native 'Indians' were living in what is now known as BC. Within a century, however, two-thirds of them had died from imported diseases.

Today there are once again about 80,000 people of native Indian ancestry living in BC. The Salish inhabit the southwest of the province (the Lower Mainland) and the southeastern part of Vancouver Island. On the west coast of Vancouver Island are the Nootka. Further north along the coast reside the Kwakiutl, Bella Coola, Tsimshian, Haida and Tlingit peoples. Almost 80 per cent of BC's land area is subject to 22 native land claims, including most of greater Vancouver. The struggle to regain self-esteem and self-reliance has been accelerating. Part of this has been the visible renaissance in the arts, in totem poles, masks, talking sticks, bent boxes, canoes, clothing and jewellery. Totem poles, the largest wood carvings known, are scattered throughout Vancouver. Some of the best are in Stanley Park, at the Museum of Anthropology and at the Capilano Suspension Bridge. Some of these carved cedar poles are memorials to the dead, others portray family trees, while still others relate mythological adventures.

Carved in a stylised realism, totem poles are sometimes difficult to decipher, but here are some of the creatures commonly seen. The thunderbird is the creator and controller of all elements and spirits. The raven is credited with providing light, fire and water. The whale symbolises strength and bravery. The bear, regarded as an elder kinsman, represents strength, authority and mobility. The eagle represents wisdom, authority and power, and the salmon abundance and prosperity.

The Orpheum: A Canadian Classic

*H*ere in one of North America's youngest cities, the patina of the past so prevalent in Europe is most wonderfully preserved in the Orpheum theatre. This gracious old building boasts a history of hosting such great artists as Charlie Chaplin, Igor Stravinsky and Helen Hayes. Its grand opening in 1927 was a social highlight in city history. The Orpheum, with 2,800 seats, was then the largest theatre on the Pacific coast. The premiere featured a silent movie, but people really came to see the vaudeville: Marie White and the Blue Slickers, dance exponents Chaney and Fox, Ethel Davis in refreshing song chatter, and everybody's favourite, Toto the clown with his little dog Whiskey.

Interior and backstage wonders

The Orpheum has always been a star, even with mediocre performers. Originally built as a link in the Chicago-based theatre chain, it was designed in conservative Spanish Renaissance style, with a basic colour scheme of antique ivory and gold. Ornamented pilasters and colonnades, highlighted with imitation and sometimes real gold-leaf, contrasted with rich tapestries of black and gold arabesques, creating an aura of exotic luxury. Dramatic maroon velvet draperies lent a regal touch. A hundred glittering chandeliers lighted the hall.

Beneath the stage, an electrically operated elevator raised and lowered three big Wurlitzer organs, which sounded like a full orchestra. One is still played a few times every year. An animal room accommodated the assortment of dogs, monkeys, tigers and elephants featured in some of the shows. An efficient ventilation system changed the air in the theatre every three minutes. One Orpheum manager said the downstairs was spooky and uncomfortably reminiscent of *The Phantom of the Opera*.

Events at the Orpheum include concerts by the Vancouver Symphony Orchestra

Famous players and the talkies

During the early 1930s, when live music faded and talking pictures took over, the Orpheum passed into the hands of Famous Players Theatres. The Nabob company sponsored elegant afternoon teas on the mezzanine.

One of the Orpheum's proudest moments was probably the Canadian première of *Gone With The Wind* in 1939. The theatre has attracted countless famous faces, including Marilyn Monroe, who came to town in 1956 to publicise *Gentlemen Prefer Blondes.*

Snack vending machines appeared in the Orpheum in 1942, and a confectionery counter in 1945. By 1950 usherettes were selling confections from trays in the auditorium. From 1943 to 1954, Nabob's Harmony House was broadcast from coast to coast from 'Canada's most beautiful theatre'. One of the last *grandes premières* was *King Rat* in 1965, with a guest appearance by author James Clavell, then living in West Vancouver.

Meanwhile the Vancouver Symphony Orchestra had been a frequent tenant from the early 1930s.

Restoration to former glory

In 1973 Famous Players announced that the Orpheum would be gutted to create six mini-cinemas, reflecting a continuing trend towards smaller theatres. Vancouverites wrote 8,500 letters in protest. Consequently, the city purchased the Orpheum for $3.9 million and spent almost as much restoring the acoustics and fine furnishings. Octogenarian artist and decorator Tony Heinsbergen, who had worked on the original structure in 1927, supervised the interior decoration and painted the

The luxuriously decorated interior of Vancouver's magnificent Orpheum Theatre

mural on the massive 20m overhead dome. Florentine Joseph Tinucci did much of the ornate and decorative plasterwork and reproduced the columns, now part of the soundshell.

In 1977, the Orpheum reopened, once again a breathtaking beauty and the finest heritage concert hall in the country. In 1983, a new foyer was completed, and the Orpheum was declared a National Historic Site. Today, the Orpheum continues to host classical and popular musical events. *Smithe Street at Seymour. Tel: 684–ARTS. Open: tours upon request.*

Science World

A hundred years ago, the site of Science World was a swamp covered with water. Today, its silver geodesic sphere is a city landmark, shimmering over the eastern end of False Creek. Billed as the most curious place on earth, this science complex attracts 700,000 inquiring minds a year.

Most visitors like to spend two to three hours at Science World, and many enjoy lunch or a snack in the Bytes Cafeteria before moving on. In the street-level foyer are the Information Centre, cloakrooms, telephones, and the cafeteria and gift shop.

Scientific wonders discovered

On the street level beyond the entrance are the Gravitram for experimenting with potential energy and the force of gravity; the IBM InfoWindows, which introduce the world of computers, and the puzzling optical effects of the Visual Illusions exhibit.

On the second level, the Matter and Forces exhibition presents the world of physics, where visitors can touch a tornado, lose their shadows and stretch an echo. The nearby Search Gallery focuses on the natural history of BC. There are tree roots hanging from the ceiling, a crawl-through beaver lodge, a hollow tree and a see-through beehive.

The Music Machines Gallery allows the inquisitive literally to step on sound and compose music on a giant walk-on synthesiser which can be programmed for 120 sound selections. Everyone has fun playing in booths filled with keyboards, drum pads and an assortment of electronic instruments demonstrating the physics of sound.

In the Travelling Exhibits Gallery, interactive exhibits which change

At night the futuristic dome of Science World is a spectacular city landmark

1455 Quebec Street,
across from the Main
Street SkyTrain
station.
Tel: 687–7832.
Open: Sunday to
Friday 10am–5pm,
Saturday 10am–9pm .
Admission charge.

*Mysteries of science
are entertainingly
unravelled for visitors
to Science World*

regularly include kaleidoscopes, challenging puzzles with tangrams (Chinese puzzles which consist of several basic shapes which can be combined to form a great variety of other figures) and geometric shapes; the study of physiognomy, in which the curious can observe how faces express feeling, deceive, encode identity and record experiences; and Jim Henson's *Muppets*. At the Science Theatre, the most popular shows are the Arcs and Sparks electricity show and the laser light presentation.

Big-screen excitement

The third level at Science World houses the 400-seat OMNIMAX Theatre where the audience is surrounded with awesome images on the world's largest domed screen and engulfed in wrap-around sound. These larger-than-life shows cover such subjects as the history of transportation, the vast icy wilderness of Antarctica, and the explosive ring of fire circling the Pacific Rim.

Programmes for children

Science World organises weekend workshops for children aged from five to 12, with opportunities for hands-on experimentation under the guidance of some 70 staff members and 130 volunteers.

Designed to put youngsters in touch with the discoveries of technology and science, the sessions cover such topics as force fields, floaters and sinkers, worms and insects, astronomy and electronics.

Stanley Park

*I*n a province so vast and varied as BC, there are many close-to-nature hideaways. But it is relatively rare to find an urban wilderness so accessible to so many people as Stanley Park. About a 10-minute walk from downtown, the park covers an area of 400 hectares (about the same size as Central Park in New York City), jutting northward into Burrard Inlet and marking the entrance to Vancouver Harbour. Surrounding it is a 10km seawall popular with walkers and cyclists.

From wilderness to park
Remarkable foresight on the part of Vancouver's city council in 1886 resulted in the creation of Stanley Park. The swampy peninsula was then a naval

A Stanley Park squirrel on alert for food

reserve where deer, bear, racoon and cougar roamed along narrow trails and abandoned logging roads. The council petitioned the federal government to set it aside as a park.

The petition was granted, leaving only Deadman's Island as a naval base. So in 1888, the then Governor General of Canada, Lord Stanley, dedicated the park 'to the use and enjoyment of people of all colours, creeds and customs for all time'.

A park for all tastes
Today, about eight million people a year come from all over Canada and the world to enjoy Stanley Park. But there is still enough of nature for everyone. Even on a warm summer day, visitors who do not want to mingle with the crowds can seek out the solitude of a shady trail.

Stanley Park is many things to many people. To youngsters, it is the sandy beach, a baby beluga whale or a miniature railway. To teenagers, it is a trysting place and a playground for such sports as soccer, skateboarding and cycling. To families, the park often means a Sunday picnic on a blanket under weeping willows. To the many elderly who live near by in the West End concrete jungle, this urban oasis means a pleasant stroll around Lost Lagoon to feed the birds and squirrels.

The green oasis

The dense park forest consists mainly of cool conifers – red cedar, Douglas fir and hemlock. One old red cedar here measures 6m across and 64m high. The deciduous underforest is mostly of broad-leafed maples, vine maples and alders. The cultivated Rose Garden, which displays thousands of blooms every summer, adds a big splash of colour near the Georgia Street park entrance.

Park wildlife

There are few wild animals in the park today, except for those in the zoo and aquarium. The last cougar disappeared nearly 50 years ago. Occasionally a black-tailed deer swims over from the North Shore to chat with his enclosed cousins through the fence and maybe enjoy a free lunch.

The beavers have been removed from Beaver Lake, because their efficient sawmill and logging operations were destroying many trees and leaving others to fall on unsuspecting visitors. They also dug tunnels that undermined the miniature railway and penetrated the bison pen. After Easter every year, a suspicious number of domestic bunnies appear in the park, suggesting that some parents have given their kiddies more than they can handle.

It was migratory birds, however, that introduced carp to the Lost Lagoon, named by poetess Pauline Johnson when its waters used to disappear at low tide. The water now locked in by man-made devices is fresh. The Lost Lagoon area is a bird sanctuary, home to cormorants, mergansers, scaup, ringbill, green wing-tail, shovelers, mallard and many other

Vancouverites take advantage of Stanley Park's green space for outdoor family fun

species of feathered friends.

A few hundred Canada geese also maintain residence here and another thousand or so fly in for the winter. In spring, mother geese, ducks and swans parade proudly around with their gaggles of young ones.

Bald eagles, which have several nests in the park, fly over Lost Lagoon and, on occasions, shamelessly grab an unsuspecting mallard for a meal, totally indifferent to horrified onlookers who have forgotten that Mother Nature is both creative and cruel.

Stanley Park Zoo

*T*he Stanley Park Zoo was born as the result of an incident about a century ago. Shortly after the park opened in 1889, the park warden adopted a black bear, which he kept tethered to a tree stump. Apparently, the local vicar's wife used to bring over household scraps to feed the bear. But one day the bear ignored the food and took a swipe at the lady's skirt, ripping part of it away with his claws. So the bear was banished to a bear pit, and it was decided to set aside an enclosed section of the park for wild animals. Since then, the zoo has grown to house some 400 animals representing 90 different species.

Today, about 2 million people a year visit the bear grottoes, penguin playground, otter pool, monkey house and the aviary, which includes bats, all in the lower zoo. In the upper zoo, Arctic wolves, bison, deer, emus, kangaroos and beaver live mostly in open-air enclosures, while peacocks and other exotic birds roam freely.

The nearby Children's Zoo affords a great opportunity for youngsters to hug and be nuzzled by dozens of domestic animals. This 'petting zoo' includes, as well as the usual rabbits and goats, such unusual species as Jacob sheep, Vietnamese pot-bellied pigs and miniature cows, along with various reptiles and birds.

The adjacent Miniature Railway, which has always carried more adults than children, was built about 30 years ago, partly because terrific winds had uprooted thousands of trees and created an open area. Passengers ride in little canopied coaches pulled by a replica of the engine that led the first transcontinental train in to Vancouver in 1887. The 10-minute ride along the narrow rails goes through an avalanche tunnel past wild animal exhibits and round a small artificial lake.

Tel: 681–1141. Open: 10am–dusk. The main zoo is free; but there is an admission charge to the Children's Zoo and the Miniature Railway.

VANCOUVER AQUARIUM
The Vancouver Aquarium is home to more than 9,000 aquatic creatures. A 5.5m-high bronze sculpture of a leaping killer whale, expertly crafted by Haida artist Bill Reid, marks the entrance.

Inside the aquarium, the more active denizens of the deep range from delicate sea-horses and smiling crocodiles to playful sea otters and the sleek killer whales that Reid so beautifully portrayed.

The Marine Mammal Deck is a great place for watching the orcas swim, socialise and play. Near by a wall-size viewing window shows playful sea otters cavorting above and below water. On the same deck is another area for harbour seals.

The Arctic Canada exhibition lets visitors look beneath the polar ice of the High Arctic at graceful white beluga whales; the big underwater windows are fine for nose-to-nose viewing. Other sights and sounds of the far north, including fish with antifreeze genetically

built in, are presented in a discovery centre.

The North Pacific Gallery and the Rufe Gibbs Hall have displays of such Canadian coastal water residents as giant octopuses, silvery salmon and waving sea anemones.

The humid Amazon Gallery provides pathways for strolling through a small tropical jungle, with banana and other equatorial trees where sloths hang lazily in the heat. Brightly coloured tropical birds flit among the tiny marmosets living in the tree-tops. Other imported Amazon residents include anacondas, piranhas, sting rays and electric eels.

The Tropical Gallery features steely-eyed sharks, fish that glow in the dark, and rainbows of reef fishes whose

White beluga whales never fail to draw attention at the Vancouver Aquarium

families come from the clear blue waters of the Caribbean and Australia's Great Barrier Reef.

Children especially enjoy the tidal pools where they can touch anemones, chitons, and star fishes. School children frequently tour the zoo and aquarium on weekday mornings, so the afternoon is usually a less crowded time to visit.

The aquarium's Summer Speakers' Series offers early evening lectures by naturalists on a variety of topics. *Stanley Park. Tel: 682–1118. Open: mid-June to early September 9.30am–9pm, mid-October to mid-March 10am–5pm, rest of the year 10am–6pm. Admission charge.*

Unknown Vancouver

*A*lthough Vancouverites love their city, they sometimes take local treasures for granted, so visitors have to hunt to find them. Such local newspapers as the *Georgia Strait*, along with local radio and television stations, provide information on the area's life and leisure. Almost every weekend sees a variety of community events. At the spring dog parade, hundreds of Vancouverites walk their pets in Stanley Park. Libraries often hold readings by Canadian authors, and visitors may purchase a temporary card to borrow books.

Juicy, ripe salmonberries are a tempting sight in British Columbia's countryside in summer

For an outdoor adventure, try picking strawberries, raspberries and blueberries in the Fraser Valley in summer. Salmonberries and blackberries can also be picked along many country roads and trails.

A great way to see the suburbs is to take in a garage sale on a Saturday or Sunday morning: this combines the opportunity for a bargain buy with an ideal informal meeting place. It is interesting to see what people sell and buy. No one is in a hurry and it is easy to strike up conversations. And you may get your Christmas shopping done early and at reduced prices.

CAPILANO FISH HATCHERY
Here you can watch salmon in various stages of growth in glass-fronted holding tanks. In the spawning season, the fish swim upstream and leap ladders into the hatchery.
Off Capilano Road in North Vancouver. Tel: 666–1790. Open: daily 8am–dusk.

NATIONAL FILM BOARD
The National Film Board's library hires out 1,000 Canadian video tapes, varying from animated shorts to profiles of Canadian poets and lengthy documentaries. An invaluable source of information for film and video buffs.
1045 Howe Street. Tel: 666–0716. Open: daily 9am–5pm.

VANCOUVER FLEA MARKET
Bargain shopping is a favourite pastime in Vancouver – as can be seen at the suburban garage sales – and the flea market is a mecca for junk-hunters. Vancouverites reveal their hidden treasures at this weekend event, where both junk and genuine bargains fill the display tables.
703 Terminal Avenue. Tel: 685–0666 . Open: Saturday and Sunday 9am–5pm. Admission charge.

Yaletown

Yaletown, the trendiest downtown area, centres around Mainland Street between Nelson and Davie streets. Just over a century ago, this neighbourhood was rainforest wilderness – until 1887, when the Canadian Pacific Railway moved its operations from the little town of Yale to this spot on the north shore of False Creek. A shanty town of wood-frame homes, boarding houses and hotels developed here. One of the original wooden homes, the Perry Linden House, still stands at 1021 Richards Street.

After the turn of the century, brick warehouses replaced the wooden structures. By the 1950s most residents had moved to the suburbs. In recent years, creative people have been converting the old warehouses into work and retail space, resulting in wonderful walking streets of shops, galleries and restaurants.

At entrepreneur Johni de Groot's Sample Room, at 1000 Mainland Street, a discount clothing store, restaurant, coffee bar, confectionery and card shop, and hair studio all flow into each other under one roof.

The Yaletown Galleria, at 1080 Mainland, houses three floors of offices and shops, overlooking a central atrium. The shops include the Light Resource, where a lighting specialist makes

cappuccinos for customers, and the Five Continents Trading Company, which sells furniture and accessories ranging from étagères to oriental urns.

Il Barino Bistro, at 1116 Mainland, recently voted Vancouver's favourite restaurant, features both Italian cuisine and décor.

A couple of doors away, the Sergio Bustamente Gallery displays the whimsical sculptures and jewellery of the Chinese-Mexican artist.

Yaletown is not too glossy – yet. It is the kind of place where an advertising executive in a Gucci jacket might carry work home in a dustbin bag. Enjoy it quickly, before it changes.

There is plenty to catch the eye at a flea market in Yaletown, as elsewhere

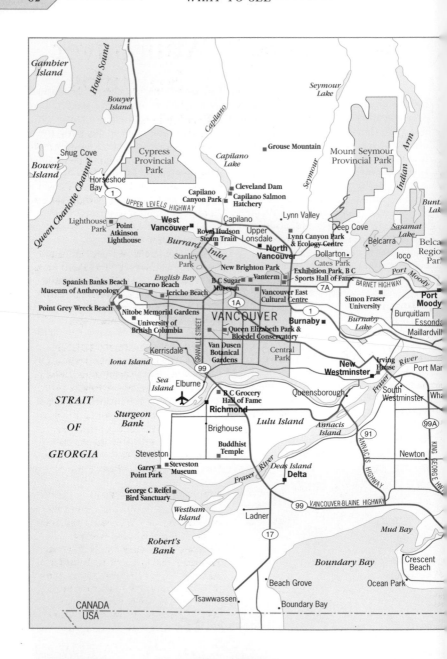

Gambier
Island

Howe Sound

Seymour
Lake

Bowyer
Island

Grouse Mountain

Mount Seymour
Provincial Park

Snug Cove

Cypress
Provincial
Park

Capilano
Lake

Capilano

Bowen
Island

Horseshoe
Bay

1

Cleveland Dam
Capilano Salmon
Hatchery

Indian Arm

Bunt...

Sasamat
Lake

Belca...
Regio...
Par...

UPPER LEVELS HIGHWAY

Capilano
Canyon Park

Queen Charlotte Channel

Lighthouse
Park

Point
Atkinson
Lighthouse

West
Vancouver

Capilano

Royal Hudson
Steam Train

Lynn Valley

Upper
Lonsdale

Deep Cove

Belcarra

loco

Burrard

North
Vancouver

Lynn Canyon Park
& Ecology Centre

Dollarton

Cates Park

Port Moody

Stanley
Park

New Brighton Park

English Bay

Inlet

Vanterm

B C Sugar
Museum

Exhibition Park, B C
Sports Hall of Fame

7A

BARNET HIGHWAY

Port
Moody

Spanish Banks Beach
Museum of Anthropology

Locarno Beach
Jericho Beach

Vancouver East
Cultural Centre

1

Simon Fraser
University

Burquitlam

Essonda...

Point Grey Wreck Beach

Nitobe Memorial Gardens

1A

VANCOUVER

Burnaby

Burnaby
Lake

Maillardvill...

University of
British Columbia

Queen Elizabeth Park &
Bloedel Conservatory

Kerrisdale

GRANVILLE STREET

Van Dusen
Botanical
Gardens

Central
Park

Iona Island

99

Sea
Island

Elburne

New
Westminster

Irving
House

River

Port Mar...

STRAIT

Sturgeon
Bank

B C Grocery
Hall of Fame

Richmond

Queensborough

Fraser

South
Westminster

Wha...

OF

Brighouse

Lulu Island

Annacis
Island

91

99A

GEORGIA

Steveston

Buddhist
Temple

Newton

KING GEORGE HWY

Garry
Point Park

Steveston
Museum

Fraser River

Deas Island

Delta

ANNACIS HIGHWAY

George C Reifel
Bird Sanctuary

Westham
Island

99

VANCOUVER-BLAINE HIGHWAY

Ladner

Mud Bay

17

Robert's
Bank

Boundary Bay

Crescent
Beach

Beach Grove

Ocean Park

CANADA
USA

Tsawwassen

Boundary Bay

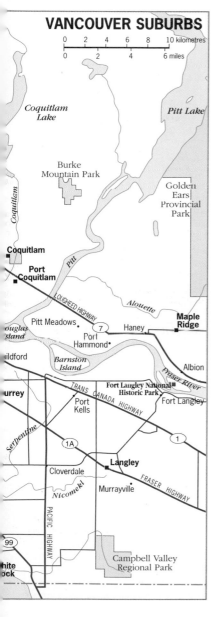

VANCOUVER SUBURBS

0 2 4 6 8 10 kilometres
0   2   4   6 miles

Coquitlam
Lake

Pitt Lake

Burke
Mountain Park

Golden
Ears
Provincial
Park

Coquitlam

Coquitlam

**Port
Coquitlam**

Pitt

LOUGHEED HIGHWAY

Alouette

Pitt Meadows

**Maple
Ridge**

ouglas
sland

7

Haney

Port
Hammond

uildford

*Barnston
Island*

Albion

Fraser River

urrey

TRANS CANADA HIGHWAY

Fort Langley National
Historic Park

Fort Langley

Port
Kells

1

Serpentine

1A

Langley

Cloverdale

FRASER HIGHWAY

Nicomekl

Murrayville

PACIFIC HIGHWAY

99

hite
ock

Campbell Valley
Regional Park

Vancouver Suburbs

STEVESTON

A half-hour drive (32km) south from downtown Vancouver is Steveston, at the mouth of the mighty Fraser. The river boasts the biggest salmon run in North America, and Steveston is home to the largest fleet of commercial fishing vessels on Canada's West Coast.

GARRY POINT PARK

A five-minute walk west from Steveston, lies sandy, wind-swept Garry Point Park. A tiny Oriental garden, beside the broad walking path, commemorates the arrival of the first Japanese immigrants to Canada more than a century ago.

AROUND MONCTON STREET

Moncton Street sports several seafood restaurants, marine supply stores, antique shops and such shopping delights as The Country Mouse, which stocks a selection of Canadian crafts. For art lovers, there is the Canoe Pass gallery, which sells traditional Coast Indian art, and the Raymond Chow Gallery, which displays work by the owner and other artists.

STEVESTON MUSEUM

Located on the town's main street, this well-known museum houses an interesting array of archive photos and a collection of everyday fishing, farming, blacksmith and domestic tools used by the early Japanese settlers. Some rooms in the two-storey 1906 structure have been restored with period furniture.
3811 Moncton Street. Open: Monday to Saturday 9.30am–1pm, 1.30pm–5pm.

North Shore

*A*cross Burrard Inlet and English Bay lies Vancouver's North Shore, backed by the rugged Coast Range mountains. Rivers, creeks and canyons meander down forested slopes, cut through clusters of houses, high-rises and businesses, and terminate along park-lined shores. Scenic coastal and mountain drives, a dozen shopping areas, a few hotels, 250 restaurants and other businesses cater to the 200,000 North Shore residents and a much greater number of visitors.

Cypress, Grouse and Seymour mountains, visible from almost every vantage point in Vancouver, dominate the scene. So near yet so far from downtown, these city mountains provide

The Skyride offers magnificent views as it whisks passengers up Grouse Mountain

a recreational paradise, particularly for picnics and hiking in summer and skiing in winter. When the clouds disperse, various vantage points provide spectacular views of downtown, the Gulf Islands, the American San Juan Islands and the eternal snows of distant Mount Baker.

THE CAPILANO RIVER AND GROUSE MOUNTAIN

Grouse Mountain, 1,220m high, is a mere 15 minutes by car from downtown Vancouver to the big parking lot below the Skyride. The aerial gondola then takes 10 minutes to transport 100 passengers at a time up through sweeping vistas to fresh crisp mountain air, winding trails, alpine meadows and a superb ski area.

The most developed of the city mountains, Grouse offers a variety of top options. You can hop on a helicopter *(tel: 683–4354)* and fly high across Capilano Canyon and between the peaks of The Lions. Or you can enjoy such other attractions as horse-drawn wagon rides, an adventure playground for the children, the Bistro Patio for relaxing, the elegant Grouse Nest Restaurant for high dining and, in July, the hang-gliding championships, when flyers jump off the mountain and glide down towards

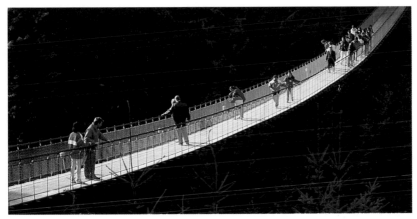

*A walk across the swaying high Capilano
Suspension Bridge is a unique experience*

the city. A 60-minute show at the
mountain-top Theatre In The Sky tells a
high-tech tale of a First Nation carver
mystically transformed into an eagle, and
of Vancouver's change from a frontier
outpost to a thriving metropolis in less
than a century.

On the way down the mountain on
Capilano Road, there are several stops
worth making. The enormous Cleveland
Dam, built about 40 years ago, divides
part of the river to create Capilano Lake,
which provides the water supply for the
city. At the Capilano Salmon Hatchery
(tel: 987–1400) from July to October,
returning salmon leap ladders into the
hatchery, and a display shows coho,
steelhead and chinook in various stages
of development.

The Capilano Suspension Bridge, the
world's oldest suspension footbridge, was
originally built in 1889. The wire rope
and wood structure sways to and fro 70m
above the rushing waters of the river
below. The bridge stretches 137m across
the steep canyon, providing access

to nature trails meandering through an
old-growth forest. Stop for a snack at the
Bridge Restaurant across the street,
where the benevolent and playful spirit of
a former resident sometimes entertains.

THE LEGEND OF THE TWO SISTERS

Renamed The Lions by the British,
these twin peaks rise to 1,646m at
the northern end of the Cypress
Provincial Park wilderness, like
sentinels guarding this sunset coast.
A long time ago, as a great Capilano
chief prepared to celebrate the
coming of age of his twin daughters,
a powerful northerly tribe
demanded war. But the daughters
persuaded their father to invite the
hostile Indians to their feast. They
accepted, and this potlatch of peace
brought brotherhood to both tribes.
In appreciation, the chief decided to
make his daughters immortal. So he
lifted them to these lofty twin peaks
to stand forever as symbols of peace
and brotherhood.

Backyard Safari

Vancouver has wonderful pockets of wilderness, both public and private. Back gardens, often hidden by trees and shrubbery, still attract some animals that once roamed here freely before people arrived. So visitors staying with friends and relatives may see wildlife by simply stepping outside or looking out of the window.

Occasionally, black bears and coyotes wander into back gardens looking for food, especially on the North Shore. At least one cougar who lost his trail map ended up in the concrete jungle by mistake not long ago. But the creatures most commonly seen in the city are such small mammals as squirrels, chipmunks, skunks and racoons.

Squirrels, some brown, some black, some grey, are active during the day, usually hunting for coniferous seeds. Since they do not hibernate, they usually hide away cones for winter use. Squirrels often scold and chatter to assert territorial boundaries as do chipmunks.

Chipmunks, however, are much smaller than squirrels. They dart rather than run, and have black and white bands on their backs and faces. Most squirrels and chipmunks around Lost Lagoon in Stanley Park are used to being hand-fed by West End residents.

Local skunks are about 0.5m long and have black coats with white stripes on the back, and bushy tails with white tips. Because skunks are nocturnal, they are rarely seen, which is probably fortunate. One of the few antidotes to the strong smelly secretion they eject when disturbed is a bath in tomato juice.

Racoons, also nocturnal, are larger than skunks, have greyish fur, a bushy tail with four to six black rings and a black mask around the eyes. Like black bears, they are good tree climbers. Their dextrous front paws are excellent for opening both clams and rubbish bins. Although racoons can be easily tamed, they are fierce fighters when cornered.

Racoons, usually asleep by day, are busy food hunters at dead of night

The humble spider's web provides an attractive element to any garden

Scampering squirrels are commonly seen residents of Vancouver's leafy areas

NORTH SHORE MOUNTAINS

CYPRESS PROVINCIAL PARK

Northwest of Vancouver, overlooking Howe Sound to the west, Cypress Provincial Park provides spectacular views over the city to Mount Baker and southwest to Vancouver Island and the Gulf Islands. Excellent cross-country ski trails and good downhill runs attract Vancouverites every day and evening in winter. In summer, the main attraction is the network of hiking trails. Some, such as the Yew Lake circuit, are suitable for novices, while the Crest Trail challenges the experts.

It takes about 20 minutes to drive to the park along the Cypress Parkway from the exit on Upper Levels Highway

Canada's emblem, the maple tree makes a gorgeous display of colour in autumn

(Highway 1/99). The end of the road is marked by a large parking area, a cafeteria, a shop and the park administration building, where brochures illustrating the trails are available.

The forest comprises mostly evergreens, such as Douglas and amabilis fir, which thrive on this rainy coast. Deciduous trees include alders, maples, and the flowering dogwood, whose neat white blossom is the provincial flower. Ferns and mosses, fed by stumps and fallen and ageing trees, flourish, and marsh marigold, skunk cabbage and salmonberries also brighten the landscape. Black bears love the berries, so be sure to give them right of way. Watchful eyes sometimes see deer feeding on the open slopes along the road. The boldest bird is the whisky jack, which lands right on picnic tables, while chickadees, nuthatches, crossbills and Steller's jays forage in the forest.

MOUNT SEYMOUR PROVINCIAL PARK

This park encompasses 3,500 hectares of wilderness, including Mount Elsay and Mount Bishop, as well as Mount Seymour (1,450m). It contains old-growth fir, western red and yellow cedar and hemlock, with carpets of alpine flowers in open areas. Coyotes and deer appear at times close to the highway, and hares, Douglas squirrels and martens sometimes skirt the hiking trails. An occasional black bear or cougar is sometimes sighted in the back country. The guided tours and displays in the Seymour Demonstration Forest (tel: 432–6286) are an excellent way to learn about local flora and fauna, rainforests and fisheries.

The winding 13km highway up Seymour ends at parking lot 4, near the cafeteria and chair lift. The Goldie Lake/Flower Lake Trail, a nordic ski route in winter, provides an easy and relatively flat one-hour loop, although a dozen other recommended walks are

Black bears are sometimes seen in wilder parts of Mount Seymour Provincial Park

listed in the brochure available in the cafeteria. Part-way down the highway, a two-hour walk along the Baden-Powell Trail leads down through thick forest and across ravines to the village of Deep Cove, on Indian Arm, which has a sandy beach and a canoe rental shop near by.

Parks on Indian Arm

A water taxi runs across Indian Arm from Deep Cove to Belcarra Regional Park, which shelters Sasamat Lake, one of the warmest in the region. Cates Park, where the waters of Indian Arm and Burrard Inlet meet, is popular with scuba divers. A 15m-long war canoe carved in an unusual chequerboard design is displayed in the park. The nearby Malcolm Lowry Walk provides a peaceful 10-minute stroll through the leafy forest and back along the shell-strewn shore.

West Vancouver

*M*ention West Vancouver and most Canadians conjure up images of sprawling million-dollar waterfront mansions backed by park-like gardens, and patio drives filled with Mercedes and Jaguars. It is true that the municipality's 40,000 residents do boast the highest per capita income in Canada. But many small clapboard cottages, built as summer homes long before the Guinness family built the Lions Gate Bridge in 1938, still survive here untouched by developers. These older houses, most worth less than $50,000, sit on lots currently valued at $300,000. About 20 per cent of West Vaners are pensioned senior citizens.

West Vancouver is not the Wild West. There is little crime and no industry. The suburb snakes for 20km along the north shore of English Bay from the bridge to Horseshoe Bay and climbs, at most, 5km up the slope towards Cypress Mountain. Although there are 60 public parks for 15,000 homes, most back gardens would look like parks to New Yorkers. Once people have lived here, they say there is nowhere else in Canada they would want to live, even though commuters encounter frequent waits in

Lions Gate Bridge spans Burrard Inlet, linking downtown with the North Shore

The old lighthouse at Lighthouse Park still guides ships along Burrard Inlet

summer to cross the bridge to the big city.

For browsing or buying, West Vancouver has the Park Royal Shopping Centre and a good range of little stores in Ambleside village and in the one block between 24th and 25th Street called Dundarave. Here shops vary from the practical Home Hardware store to elegant recycled clothing boutiques.

Visitors can also enjoy fishing, golfing, tennis at free public courts, lawn bowling, swimming and exercise at several fitness circuits.

FERRY BUILDING
Built in 1913, this heritage building, which now serves as a waterfront gallery for local arts, was once a meeting place for residents arriving from and leaving for downtown Vancouver. The adjacent waterfront park, known as Ambleside Landing, offers a view of Prospect Point in Stanley Park, and features a fountain sculpture and a fishing pier complete with cleaning table.

1414 Argyle Avenue. Tel: 925–3605. Open: 11am–dusk.

GERTRUDE LAWSON MUSEUM
This old ballast-stone house was built in 1940 by Gertrude Lawson, daughter of the Father of West Vancouver, businessman John Lawson. It is now a museum relating the history of the area. The unusual stone façade of the house echoes the architectural character of the grand homes of Scotland which Ms Lawson greatly admired. The stones are believed to have come from New Zealand as ballast on timber trading ships.
680 17th Street. Tel: 926–9254. Open: 11am–dusk. Admission charge.

Parks and walkways
Gardens, parks and walkways are everywhere here. Ambleside Park is a great place to see residents walking their dogs. The spectacular 2km paved Seawalk has a fenced-off trail for four-footed friends. The best beach is the little one near Dundarave Pier, where a concession stand serves the best cheeseburgers in BC. Westward, a pebbled shore strewn with driftwood is a great place for beachcombing. Caulfield Park, which has a forested path along the waterfront, is famous for its flush toilets!

Lighthouse Park, a treasure hidden away further west along Marine Drive, has a labyrinth of trails through an enchanted forest of giant Douglas firs, pines, hemlocks, and arbutus trees recognisable by their smooth, peeling rust-red bark. The Point Atkinson Lighthouse, built in 1912, is one of the few working lighthouses left in the province. The promontory just west of the lighthouse offers views of freighters anchored in English Bay, Point Grey and the mountains of Vancouver Island.

Lower Mainland

Recollections of the past – wooden barrels being made in the old cooperage at historic Fort Langley

FORT LANGLEY

An hour's drive east from Vancouver's chrome and glass high-rises is the historic little village of Fort Langley, the site of the original fort and fur-trading post where BC began. It was here that BC was declared a Crown colony in 1858.

Fort Langley village has, so far, escaped the contrived charm which often accompanies historical reconstructions. Its quaint clapboard churches, antique shops and false-fronted buildings are mostly original.

Near the fort, the BC Farm Museum houses a comprehensive collection of steam tractors, stump pullers, ploughs, reapers, harvesters, buckboards, a working sawmill and a vintage Tiger Moth plane, the first crop duster in the province.

The Langley Centennial Museum, next door, displays numerous Coast Salish Indian artefacts and a selection of 19th-century pioneer crafts and furnishings.

Fort Langley National Historic Park

First built in 1827, Fort Langley was once the Hudson's Bay Company's most important provisioning post in the Pacific Northwest, and has been reconstructed to re-create the past. Within the palisaded high wooden walls, the Big House, the bastion, a cooperage and carpentry shop, and a blacksmith's forge have been rebuilt. The storehouse, the only original structure on site, is stacked with furs, clothing, trapping equipment, trading goods and other supplies used by fur traders, gold miners, Indians, and other 19th-century residents.

Interpreters in period costumes demonstrate pioneer life at the fort. Some are blacksmiths fashioning tools; some are coopers building barrels, which were once used to ship salmon and other foodstuffs from the fort; and some bake salmon and bannock in open outdoor ovens for visitors to sample. Other interpreters present talks and organise games so that visiting children can enjoy learning local history. Coast Salish Natives from the neighbouring MacMillan Island band often work at the fort constructing canoes, carving paddles and making jewellery.

The Big House replicates the original building which was pulled down in 1886. The refurbished parlour suggests the relative luxury the chief trader and his family enjoyed, and an intriguing diary displayed in the big hall describes early life at the fort.

Brigade Days, held in early August, re-enacts the fur brigades arriving to trade at Fort Langley after weeks of canoeing south through networks of rivers. Douglas Day, in mid-November, is another colourful ceremony, which

The Community Hall, one of many clapboard buildings at quaint Fort Langley village

THE HUDSON'S BAY COMPANY

This company of adventurers was an English corporation formed in 1670, during the reign of King Charles II, to trade in North America throughout the lands that drained into Hudson's Bay.

The commercial empire that grew out of it began with a few shiploads of British goods being traded for furs, and eventually covered more than 10 per cent of the surface of the earth. After numerous dramatic struggles, a merger with the North West Company took place in 1821.

When Canada became a country 125 years ago, the Hudson's Bay Company gave up its trade monopoly, but retained its forts and trading posts. Eventually a chain of Hudson's Bay department stores was built in Western Canada and still exists today. Small Bay stores remain as the commercial centres of several remote settlements scattered throughout the Canadian Arctic.

commemorates the inauguration of BC.

The Friends of the Fort gift shop stocks a variety of souvenirs, including reproductions of old trading goods from the fort. *The fort is open daily from 10am to 4pm, with extended hours in summer. Admission charge.*

The Native riverboat trip

A pleasant way to visit Fort Langley is aboard *The Native*, a working replica of a late 19th-century paddlewheeler. This 100-passenger vessel follows the Fraser River upstream from New Westminster to Fort Langley. The four-hour journey traces the route taken by fortune hunters, fur traders, miners, merchants, millionaires and stage-coach robbers during the last century. Native Indians also canoed the route while fishing, hunting and trapping. The excursion is narrated, with extracts by early explorers, and includes a buffet lunch. *20465 Douglas Crescent, Langley. Tel: 525–4465. Open: daily, May to October. Boarding 9.30am; return 4pm. Admission charge.*

Harrison Hot Springs

*T*hese hot springs were discovered rather dramatically during the 1850s when a clumsy prospector was tipped out of his canoe into Harrison Lake. He was dumbfounded to find the water not frigid, but warm. Word spread and, for later prospectors on the gold rush trail, Harrison Hot Springs became a popular stop-over site.

Although Harrison Hot Springs Hotel is today in the luxury category, anyone can enjoy such specialities as lobster mousse or poached salmon in the restaurant and look out at the lake. There is also plenty of less expensive hotel, motel and campground accommodation. Other restaurants line the lakeshore.

Shoppers and browsers can enjoy a range of shops offering everything from video rentals, camping supplies and Canadiana to the Christmas decorations sold year-round in the cosy Holly Tree Place.

Soothing spring waters

Two springs percolate from the base of nearby mountains. A sulphur spring, about two-thirds sodium sulphate and sodium chloride, flows out at 68°C. A potash spring, with potassium chloride and sodium sulphate making up more than half its mineral content, enters the lake at 71°C. Both spring waters also contain lime and magnesium sulphates, sulphurated hydrogen and bicarbonates of lime and iron.

A pipe system carries the mineral waters to the hotel and public pools, for which there is an admission charge. The water is stored in huge tanks and cooled to 38°C, the perfect temperature for a soothing soak. Massages are available. To see the springs bubbling up from their source, walk westward along the dyke beside the lake and past the hotel.

Outdoor activities and sport

The town of Harrison Hot Springs offers a great variety of activities for outdoor lovers. Boaters enjoy exploring the lake, which stretches 60km north, but watch for strong thermal winds which may rise rapidly shortly after noon on a summer day. The morning calm is great for water-skiing, and the afternoon winds are great for windsurfing. Other outdoor options include golf, tennis, cycling, croquet, horseshoes and shuffleboard.

Numerous walking and hiking trails provide easy access to the forests and mountains. The easiest one, about 2km long, follows the lake from the Harrison Hot Springs Hotel to the boat launch and around the lagoon, while the Campbell Lake Trail, which requires more than four hours, rises a challenging 600m to a beautiful mountain lake.

The Kite Flying Festival (no admission charge) in early June and the Sandsculpture Competition in early September attract many visitors to Harrison Hot Springs every year. The Guinness record for the world's tallest sandcastle was set here in 1990.

There is a parade of gaily lighted boats on the lake during the evening of 1 July, Canada Day. The week-long Festival of the Arts, later in July, features a spectrum of artistic expression in music, dance, theatre and visual art and artefacts. A special day set aside for

children includes story-tellers, face-painting, workshops and other activities, and a writers' evening offers readings and discussions with Canadian authors.

MINTER GARDENS

Tucked away a few metres west off Yale Road, just after the turn-off north from Highway 1 to Harrison Hot Springs, are the Minter Gardens. Gentle pathways wind through 11 hectares of sights, sounds, fragrances, textures and tastes. In springtime, tulips, daffodils, hyacinths, primulas, rhododendrons and azaleas blaze with colour. Summer

Just 130km east of Vancouver, Harrison Hot Springs is a popular holiday centre

brings a prize display of annuals, and autumn presents a shower of falling leaves in green, gold and red, backdropped by the snow-dusted peaks of 2,134m Mount Cheam. Other highlights include the Rose Garden, which blossoms most of the year; topiaries of southern belles and northern deer; a rare collection of Penjing rock bonsai; and a fragrance trail for the blind. *Tel: 794–7191. Open: April to October 9am–dusk. Admission charge. Free parking.*

Peace Arch Park

*C*anada, the second largest country in area on earth (after Russia), and the US have the longest undefended international border in the world, stretching 6,500km from the Atlantic Ocean to the Pacific. Shared by both countries, the Peace Arch Park at the southern end of Highway 99 in BC may be one of the most beautiful border crossings anywhere.

A monument to peace

The idea of a peace arch was conceived by the late Samuel Hill of Seattle to commemorate a permanent peace between Canada and the US. While president of the Pacific Highway Association, Hill, a road builder and

Quaker, proposed that an arch be constructed at the centenary of the signing of the Treaty of Ghent in 1814. The treaty marked the end of the War of

The Peace Arch straddles the US-Canada border as a monument to lasting peace

1812 between Great Britain and the US, resolving the ongoing conflict between the two powers at that time. The Peace Arch, the first such structure in the world, became a reality in 1921 and marked the 300th anniversary of the sailing of the Pilgrim Fathers to America.

Built of concrete reinforced with steel, in Greek Doric style, the arch was designed to vibrate but not crack in case of an earthquake. The gleaming white open portal, which stands about 30m high, flies the Canadian and American flags side by side. Across the top on the American side is the inscription 'Children of a Common Mother'. The Canadian side reads 'Brethren Dwelling Together in Unity'.

Two iron gates span the opening that leads from one country to the other. Here children and adults from both countries like to stand, with one foot planted on Canadian soil, the other in the US. In a celebration held in early June every year, children from both countries meet here and file through the portal and exchange flags. Over the west gate is written '1814 Open for One Hundred Years – 1914' and over the east 'May These Gates Never Be Closed'.

Originally incorporated into the Canadian side was a beam from the SS _Beaver_, which in 1836 became the first steamship to enter the Pacific Ocean. A beam of wood from the hull of _The Mayflower_, the ship that carried the Pilgrim Fathers to America in 1621, was embedded into the American side. These relics have since been removed and stored elsewhere for future generations.

A garden of harmony
During the 1920s, some peace lovers banded together to raise funds to purchase land surrounding the Peace

Pleasant gardens surround the Peace Arch each side of the international border

Arch for a park. BC schoolchildren responded, some with only a penny, others with as much as 10 cents. More than $2,000 was raised, quite a lot in those days. The money was applied to the purchase of a portion of the property. Other funds were eventually found and 9 hectares were set aside as the Peace Arch Park. The 7 hectares that make up the Washington State Peace Arch Park were eventually acquired in a similar fashion.

Today, the Peace Arch serves as a symbol to remind all passing by that neighbours can live together in harmony.

The portal is the centrepiece for the surrounding broad green lawns, flower gardens, rockeries, playgrounds, picnic areas, shelters and kitchens that have been built on both sides over the years. The Canadian side features a wooden gazebo, a lily pond and a rectangle of red and white blossoms representing the Canadian flag. To the west, a cliff overlooks the old Burlington Northern Railway line and the waters of Semiahmoo Bay, which wash the shores of both countries.

Flowers in Season

Most people think of BC as a land blanketed in greenery. The Lower Mainland region does tend to remain eternally leafy, thanks to the temperate climate and abundant rains.

It is usually March when the first crocuses, daffodils, narcissi, tulips and hyacinths burst forth. Bold umbrellas of pink unfold on Japanese cherry trees along city streets; magnolias and camellias bloom in delicate whites and pinks, and the japonica bushes open bright clusters of flowers resembling apple blossoms. Forsythia shrubs produce golden streamers and wisterias wind long tassels of purple along building walls. Yellow skunk cabbages,

Flowers in season are displayed everywhere

Bright tulips in the VanDusen Botanical Garden

which smell like they sound, brighten dank forest areas in Stanley Park.

In June, azaleas and rhododendrons, dressed in brilliant hues of pink, salmon, coral and crimson, announce the advent of summer. Roses bloom in town and country gardens, and wild lupins brighten the roadsides. Dahlias, delphiniums, phlox, asters and poppies share the summer sun with sweet peas, gladioli, freesias, zinnias, marigolds and nasturtiums, while fuchsia and busy lizzies thrive in the shade. Moss-packed hanging baskets sport trailing lobelias and verbenas, mingled with petunias and pelargoniums.

The late summer display includes snapdragons, primroses, wallflowers and Canterbury bells.

As the golden autumn leaves fall, irises, cat-tails (or reedmace) and marsh marigolds flower near ponds and lakes.

Even the grey winter is brightened by flowering plants. Clumps of white and pink heather border lawns, while window boxes appear colourful with winter pansies and curly kale. Some roses, along with the pretty blossoms of the winter-flowering plum and the yellow trumpets of winter jasmine, smile right through a short snowfall. Holly outside and poinsettias inside follow the Christmas tradition of red and green. Red-osier dogwoods, the bright yellow twigs of Siberian dogwood and clusters of bright pink berries on the spindleberry bush also liven the winter landscape.

Cheerful spring cherry blossoms

Colourful displays of looms in Butchart Gardens

Wild thistles provide nectar for all kinds of visiting butterflies

Whistler

Named after the sound of the hoary marmot, one of the first inhabitants of the area, Whistler is a top-class winter sports centre that continues to receive accolades from skiers from all over the world. But getting there is half the fun.

The Sea to Sky Highway
Appropriately called the Sea to Sky Highway, the road to Whistler fringes fiord-like Howe Sound. Here, rugged rainforest and sheer rock faces, sculpted by glaciers during the last Ice Age, ascend to meadows blanketed in summer with Indian paintbrushes and other alpine flowers and in winter with snow.

A good picnic place along the road is Porteau Cove, which also offers good swimming, snorkeling, scuba diving, boating and fishing. The Sundowner Restaurant has a superb deck for watching both seals and sunsets. At Britannia Beach, the BC Mining Museum, once the largest copper producer in the British Empire and now a National Historic Site, offers underground tours in little electric trains and an intriguing display of old mining equipment. *(Tel: 688-8735; open Wednesday to Sunday 10am–5pm mid-May to June, daily in July and August and on weekends in September.)*

The next stop should be Shannon Falls, BC's third highest waterfall, which thunders down a 335m cliff following the trail of a slithering sea serpent, according to the local legend.

A few kilometres beyond the falls, the logging town of Squamish is famous as a

At Nairn Falls, north of Whistler, the swirling Green River offers good fishing

You can travel to Whistler, located 120km north of Vancouver, by Heli-Express (tel: 266–5386), BC Rail (tel: 631 3500), Maverick Coach Lines (tel: 255–1171) or drive yourself, which takes about two hours non-stop.

Set in fine mountain scenery, Whistler Resort is a top-class holiday centre for both summer recreation and winter sports

rock-climbing centre. The Stawamus Chief, a 700m-high granite monolith, is second in size in the world, after the Rock of Gibraltar. Another hour's drive past reflecting lakes, and through small open valleys and forest, lies Whistler.

Whistler: the mountain playground
Whistler Village is nestled between twin mountain peaks, Whistler and Blackcomb, in the Coast Range. The village is a cluster of hotels, shops, condominiums, restaurants and cobbled walkways, constructed in a mixed West Coast and imitation European style.

A five-minute walk from the village square leads to the ski lifts which service the two longest vertical drops on the continent: Blackcomb, 1,609m and Whistler 1,525m. The Whistler Express gondola whisks 10 people at a time, year-round, up to the Roundhouse in 20 minutes, while two high-speed quad chair-lifts run up to Blackcomb's Rendezvous

Ridge, and equally spectacular scenery. About a quarter of the 200 downhill runs are tailored to experts, another quarter to beginners and the rest are for intermediate skiers. Cross-country trails skirt the golf course and Lost Lake.

After the warm spring sun melts the snows of winter, avid skiers head to the Horstman Glacier and share the lifts with mountain bikers, who ride down the now-gravel trails that skiers slalom in winter. Overhead, paragliders float down to the village below.

Whistler also offers an 18-hole golf course, hiking, horseback riding, canoeing, river rafting, windsurfing and fishing. Musicians, magicians, clowns, comedians and jugglers entertain every day in the streets from mid-June to September. Major festivals feature country and blues in July, classical music in August and jazz in September.

Accommodation varies from the luxurious 343-room Chateau Whistler (tel: 938–8000), the largest château-style property built in Canada for a century, to the rustic KOA Kampground (tel: 932–5181).

Gulf Islands

*A*lmost 200 islands of all shapes and sizes lie between the Lower Mainland and Vancouver Island.

Some of these Gulf Islands offer superb natural scenery, outdoor activities and good accommodation and food. The major islands are Saltspring, North and South Pender, Galiano, Mayne and Saturna. Although locals love the quiet winters, the islands are much livelier in summer when visitors come from all over the world for the spectacular water views, the balmy climate, the abundant sunshine and the gentle lifestyle.

Most of the Gulf Islands are accessible year-round via BC Ferries (tel: 669–1211) and Harbour Air (tel: 278–3478). Ferries to the islands leave Tsawwassen on the mainland 30km south of Vancouver. Many boaters prefer to visit in their own craft, finding shelter and moorage at numerous little bays throughout the islands.

Of the six inhabited Gulf Islands, Saltspring is the most developed and the most densely populated. But Mayne, which is not the principal island, is preferred by many visitors. About 8km by 5km in area, Mayne Island has only 700 year-round residents. They are mostly artists and artisans, a few business people, and others who have retired to enjoy a leisurely island lifestyle.

Like the other Gulf Islands, Mayne is mainly bays and beaches and gentle wooded hills of arbutus, Douglas fir, alder, cedar and brilliant bursts of broom, although early settlers did clear some land for farming.

Popular activities include swimming, scuba diving, fishing, canoeing, kayaking, clam digging, beachcombing, hiking and cycling.

The Gulf Islands are popular precisely because there is little organised activity. On Mayne, there are no buses, no taxis and no scuba gear nor canoe rentals.

However, the Esso service station in Miners' Bay rents 10-speed mountain bikes during June, July and August. Most Mayne roads are hilly, but asphalted. The nearby Produce Market, Trading Post and Deli packs picnic lunches.

MAYNE'S COLOURFUL PAST

While the wilderness is wonderful, Mayne Island offers a wholesome portion of history as well. Native tribes inhabited Helen Point 5,000 years ago. Evidence remains in the middens and white beaches formed from eroded clam, abalone and oyster shells.

In the late 1850s, rowdy miners stopped here *en route* from Victoria to the gold-fields of Barkerville, and some returned to enjoy the relatively mild winters. At the turn of the century, British gentry liked to spend their summers on Mayne.

The lighthouse at Georgina Point, built in 1855, still guides vessels into the eastern entrance to Active Pass. The lighthouse is open to visitors every day of the year from 1pm to 3pm (no admission charge) as is the studio of lighthouse keeper and artist Don de Rousie, who is part Haida and spends his spare time carving yellow and red cedar into classic Native red and black designs.

The best-loved country church on Mayne Island is St Mary Magdalene's, built in 1898 on a hill overlooking Active Pass. The 180kg sandstone font was carried by rowing boat from Saturna Island in 1900.

The Mayne Island Gaol is open in summer (no admission charge). Built in 1896, it is now a museum housing memorabilia from the 19th century, including remnants from the sailing barque *Zephyr* which hit the Georgina shoals and sank in 1872.

For more information on the Gulf Islands, contact Tourism Vancouver Island, 302–45 Bastion Square, Victoria, BC V8W 1J1. Tel: 382–3551.

OTHER GULF ISLANDS

GALIANO ISLAND
Fine views at Coon Bay, Bluff Park, Mt Sutil and Mt Galiano. Montague Provincial Park offers wildlife, including eagles.

Views from Mt Maxwell, Saltspring Island

PENDER ISLANDS
Beaches and coves. Driftwood Centre and craft shops at Port Washington. Wildlife, including deer.
Events: Salmon BBQ and Fish Derby, July; Art Show, Fall Fair, August.

SALTSPRING ISLAND
Art and craft galleries. Village shops and Saturday morning market at Ganges. Views at Mt Maxwell and Ruckle Provincial Park.
Events: Round the Island Race, May; Sea Capers, June; Art/Craft Exhibition, June to September; Fall Fair, September.

SATURNA ISLAND
East Point Lighthouse. Lyall Harbour pub and store. Winter Cove Marine Park. Wildlife, including ravens and wild goats.
Events: Lamb Barbecue, July.

Haida Gwaii
(Queen Charlotte Islands)

*T*he Charlottes, named Haida Gwaii by the native Haida people, comprise two main islands, Graham and Moresby, and 150 little ones, together covering an area of 9,000 sq km. They lie north of Vancouver Island and about 120km west of Prince Rupert. Frequently hidden under a grey blanket of cloud and fog, Haida Gwaii is surrounded by treacherous seas and rocks. The Cape St James weather station, hugging the southern tip of the southernmost island, is the windiest one in Canada. But it is also the warmest, thanks to soothing Kuroshio currents crossing the Pacific Ocean from Japan.

Much of empty Moresby Island is parkland, a result of efforts by Haida and other environmentalists. Although fishermen by tradition, the 2,000 Haida who live here today are celebrated for beautifully carved wooden masks, canoes, totem poles and smaller items shaped in argillite, an ebony slate mudstone. A few hundred years ago, about 8,000 Haida lived here, famed in the region as fierce warriors. But they were decimated by Caucasian diseases, probably beginning in 1774, when the first European, Juan José Pérez, sailed round the northern coast.

Grey, weathered totem poles still stand at several abandoned villages throughout these rugged isles. The most accessible is Yan, in the north of Graham Island. A visiting permit can be purchased from the local chief, who can arrange boats and guides. The Haida, who claim 10,000 years of experience, also organise tours to the South Moresby National Park Reserve Park and Ninstints (Anthony Island), site of the largest cluster of original standing totem poles in the world.

Although about 6,000 people in all now live in Haida Gwaii, there are no banks or shopping malls. The isolation and the mists have, over the years, attracted many interesting characters, some who came to the islands because they were different, and others who became different because they came to the islands.

The moss-draped forests of the Canadian Galapagos, as Haida Gwaii is sometimes called, provide a dreamy silence for the shy black-tailed deer, Roosevelt elk and black bear that live in them. On the eastern shores, where the murmuring sea washes broad crescents of pebbles and sand, loons call soulfully over the waters and bald eagles squeal overhead from shadowing stands of ancient cedar and Sitka spruce. Whales, sea lions, porpoises and puffins live off-shore. Anglers usually go home contented with catches of rock and ling cod, salmon, halibut, trout and red snapper. Fishing remains a strong industry, although logging is fast disappearing.

DELKATLA WILDLIFE SANCTUARY
Birdwatchers especially enjoy this park where more than 100 native and migrating species of birds have been spotted. They include auklets, petrels,

puffins and sandhill cranes.
On a salt marsh near Masset, Graham Island. Tel: 626–3995. Open: daily.

NAIKOON PROVINCIAL PARK
This park offers many hiking trails, including one to Tow Hill, which over-looks an agate beach and an unusual lava formation. Sitka deer and the rare Peale's peregrine falcon can be spotted here.
On the east coast between Tlell and Masset, Graham Island. Tel: 557–4390. Open: daily.

QUEEN CHARLOTTE ISLANDS MUSEUM
This museum houses argillite carvings, cedar totem poles, natural history exhibits and relics of the early European settlements. The longhouse shelters several canoes, including *Loo Taas* (Wave-eater), designed by master carver Bill Reid.
Second Beach Road, Skidegate, Graham Island. Tel: 559–4643. Open: Tuesday to Sunday 10am–5pm in summer; afternoons only in winter. Admission charge.

Canadian Airlines (tel: 279–6611) jets twice daily from Vancouver to Sandspit, on northeast Moresby Island. Car rental is expensive and getting around the islands is difficult.

BC Ferries (tel: 669–1211) make the 7-hour run from Prince Rupert to Skidegate every day in summer and three times weekly in winter.

A 20-minute ferry runs every hour or two between Moresby Island and Graham Island, where most of the relatively small choice of motels and hotels are located.

The majestic bald eagle

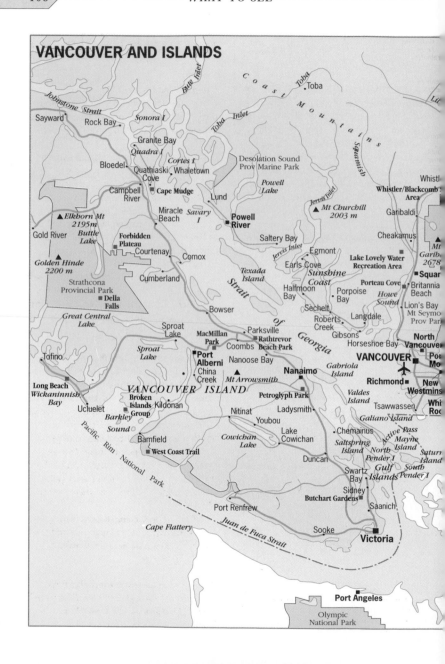

VANCOUVER AND ISLANDS

Blute Inlet

Coast Mountains

Toba Inlet

Toba

Toba

Johnstone Strait

Sayward

Rock Bay

Sonora I

Granite Bay

Quadra I

Quathiaski Cove

Cortes I

Whaletown

Bloedel

Campbell River

Cape Mudge

Lund

Squamish

Desolation Sound Prov Marine Park

Powell Lake

Whistl

Whistler/Blackcomb Area

Garibaldi

Mt Churchill 2003 m

Jervis Inlet

▲Elkhorn Mt 2195m

Gold River

Buttle Lake

Forbidden Plateau

Miracle Beach

Savary I

Powell River

Saltery Bay

Jervis Inlet

Egmont

Earls Cove

Cheakamus

Mt Garib 2678

Squar

Lake Lovely Water Recreation Area

Golden Hinde 2200 m

Courtenay

Comox

Texada Island

Sunshine Coast

Porpoise Bay

Porteau Cove

Britannia Beach

Cumberland

Strathcona Provincial Park

Della Falls

Halfmoon Bay

Sechelt

Howe Sound

Lion's Bay

Mt Seymo Prov Par

Great Central Lake

Bowser

Roberts Creek

Langdale

Gibsons

Horseshoe Bay

North Vancouver

Sproat Lake

MacMillan Park

Parksville

Rathtrevor Beach Park

Strait of Georgia

Sproat Lake

Coombs

Port Alberni

Nanoose Bay

Nanaimo

Gabriola Island

VANCOUVER

Por Mo

Tofino

China Creek

▲Mt Arrowsmith

Richmond

New Westmins

Long Beach Wickaninnish Bay

VANCOUVER ISLAND

Broken Islands Group

Kildonan

Petroglyph Park

Valdes Island

Whi Ro

Ucluelet

Barkley Sound

Nitinat

Youbou

Ladysmith

Tsawwassen

Galiano Island

Pacific

Bamfield

Cowichan Lake

Lake Cowichan

Chemainus

Saltspring Island

Mayne Island

Active Pass

Rim

West Coast Trail

Duncan

North Pender I

South Pender I

Satur Island

National

Swartz Bay

Gulf Islands

Park

Sidney

Butchart Gardens

Saanich

Port Renfrew

Cape Flattery

Juan de Fuca Strait

Sooke

Victoria

Port Angeles

Olympic National Park

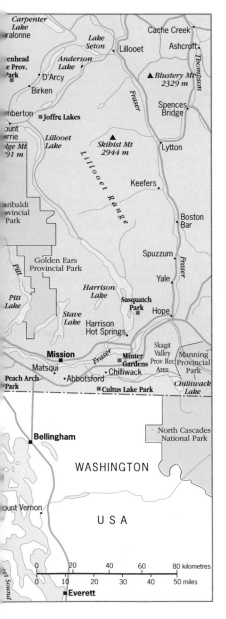

Quadra Island

Quadra Island lies off Vancouver Island's northeast coast, just a 10-minute ferry ride across Discovery Passage from the salmon-fishing centre of Campbell River.

In addition to native Indian culture and regional cuisine, the island offers many options for outdoor recreation, including kayaking, canoeing, scuba diving, whale watching and fishing.

Landlubbers can enjoy beachcombing at Rebecca Spit; hiking the trails or up Chinese Mountain for the spectacular view; and mountain biking.

For history buffs, there are interesting ruins to explore at the Lucky Jim Mine, and ancient Indian petroglyphs, or stone drawings, at Francisco Point, We-wai-kai Beach and Cape Mudge.

KWAKIUTL MUSEUM

This snail-shaped structure shelters about 300 items confiscated by the Canadian government in 1922 when they outlawed the potlatch, a ceremonial celebration where one tribe hosts another and gives them elaborate gifts.

The displays include headdresses, masks, woven cedar baskets, rattles, bent boxes, a three-storey-high totem pole and a collection of turn-of-the-century photos.

37 Weway Road, Cape Mudge. Tel: 285–3733. Open: Tuesday to Saturday 10am–4:30pm; shorter hours in winter. Admission charge.

There are regular scheduled flights from Vancouver Airport to Campbell River, and a daily floatplane service from Coal Harbour to Campbell River.

Vancouver Island

*I*slands conjure up all kinds of images, and Vancouver Island is no exception. Stretching 450km along Canada's Pacific coast, this huge island brings to mind images of mossy, dense and dark rainforests of fir, cedar and hemlock; barren, wind and surf-swept Pacific beaches; Edwardian lamp-posts draped with baskets of trailing flowers; and elegant Victorian afternoon teas.

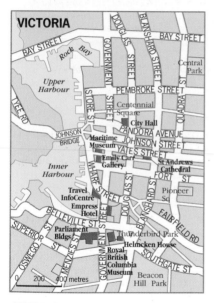

Perhaps this is because the sun shines more than in Vancouver, a mere 100km north.

With its historic buildings, colourful old Chinatown, museums, and lovely parks and gardens, Victoria offers visitors much to see and do. But for a different day, call Rent A Roadster (tel: 361–7300) and drive a 1929 Model A Ford reproduction complete with rumbleseat around the city.

Alternatively, take a harbour cruise, go fishing, or splash away a summer day at the All Fun Waterslides on Millstream Road, a 15-minute drive from the city centre (tel: 474–3184; open summer only). *For information on other attractions and activities, visit the Travel InfoCentre which is situated at 812 Wharf Street (tel: 382–2127).*

VICTORIA

BC is no longer predominantly British, as more and more people from different cultures and countries around the world continue to move here to live. But Victoria, the provincial capital, which began as a Hudson's Bay Trading Post in 1843, still retains some elements of British life – a gentle pace, traditional afternoon teas and a sense of propriety and order.

Victorians, like many island people, tend to be more relaxed and forgiving.

BUTCHART GARDENS

Possibly the most spectacular floral display on the continent today, these gardens began as an abandoned limestone quarry in 1904. Meandering paved pathways lead through 20 hectares of exquisite arrangements of more than 5,000 varieties of trees, shrubs and flowers. There is a sunken garden, rose garden, Japanese garden, Italian garden, star pond, concert lawn, fireworks basin, show greenhouse, seed store, and two restaurants and a coffee bar.

In summer, additional entertainment includes musical reviews, puppet shows, night illuminations and fireworks, while in winter, after the kaleidoscope of colourful blossoms has faded, ribbons of lights brighten the grey days. Wheel-chairs, cameras, baby pushcarts and umbrellas are available for hire.
About 21km north of Victoria via Highway 17 and Keating Cross Road. Tel: 652–5256. Open: daily 9am–dusk. Admission charge.

HELMCKEN HOUSE

Built in 1852, this historic home provides a glimpse into the life of a pioneer physician 140 years ago, and is the oldest house in BC open to the public.
Next door to the Royal BC Museum. Tel: 387–4697. Open: Thursday to Monday 11am 5pm. Admission charge.

PARLIAMENT BUILDINGS

Hourly guided tours show off this stately greystone structure and its intricate stained-glass windows, Italian marble panels, mosaic tile floors and painted murals illustrating the farming, fishing, mining and logging past of the province.

On the Inner Harbour. Tel: 387–3046. Open: Tours Monday to Friday.

ROYAL BC MUSEUM

The Royal BC Museum, which rates in many people's eyes as the finest museum in Canada, has displays of BC history which include such exhibits as a woolly mammoth, cobblestone streets bordered by Victorian storefronts, a working gold-rush waterwheel, a replica of Captain George Vancouver's ship *Discovery*, and the magical masks and totem poles of the First Nations.
675 Belleville Street. Tel: 387–3014. Open: May to September 9am–5.30pm and October to April 10am–5pm. Closed: Christmas Day. Admission charge.

THUNDERBIRD PARK

This downtown park has an outdoor display of replicas of old totem poles and original contemporary poles and carvings by coastal Indian artists.
Beside Helmcken House.

The Butchart Gardens, north of Victoria, are a showcase of floral displays.

North to Nanaimo

Spot the real people standing in front of a colourful mural at Chemainus!

'THE LITTLE TOWN THAT DID'

An hour's drive north from Victoria on the Malahat Highway (Highway 1) is the little coastal town of Chemainus. In the early 1980s, when the century-old sawmill closed and the town lay dying, a few artists began drawing larger-than-life murals on the exterior walls of buildings. Today, the town boasts Canada's largest outdoor art gallery, with 24 murals depicting the history of the Chemainus Valley. Subjects range from a 19th-century brigantine to Hong Hing's grocery store and portraits of First Nations people.

The town also has antique shops, art galleries, boutiques selling local crafts and souvenirs, and ice-cream parlours. A friendly place for lunch, although the cuisine is not cordon bleu, is Mandolino's *(tel: 246–3231)*, beside the railcar caboose InfoCentre. The annual Festival of Murals in July and August features painters and sculptors at work, puppeteers, dramatists, street dances and parades.

WAYSIDE DIVERSIONS

Three kilometres south of Nanaimo, right beside the road from Victoria, is tiny Petroglyph Park. If you blink, you might miss it. A short stroll through the woods leads to a series of ancient Indian rock carvings depicting people, birds, bottomfish and the mythical seawolf.

'THE HARBOUR CITY'

Nanaimo is best known as the 'Bathtub Capital of the World', referring to the annual mid-July festival when dozens of tubbers challenge the often choppy waters

BUNGY JUMPING

Ten kilometres south from Nanaimo is the 'Bungy Zone' (tel: 753–JUMP). For a rush of adrenalin, adventurous souls can dive off a bridge here, in the style made famous by New Zealanders, with an enormous elastic cord tied to their ankles. The cord prevents them from falling into the river 43m below, and lets them bounce up and down a few times · before being rescued by a rubber raft. The ads say bungy jumping is an all-weather sport, safe for all ages, shapes and sizes and that no special clothing or skills are required. And in case the folks back home might be sceptical, jumpers can buy a take-home video of their daring.

to race 54km across Georgia Strait to Kitsilano Beach in Vancouver. Also called 'The Harbour City', Nanaimo is a key link in the BC Ferries chain, with frequent regular sailings to and from Tsawwassen and Horseshoe Bay on the Lower Mainland.

A walking tour of the old town should include the Centennial Museum, 100 Cameron Street *(tel: 753–1821)*, which has exhibits explaining such events as the arrival of the Spanish, and discovery of coal, as well as artefacts of Vancouver Island's native peoples. The highlight of the area is The Bastion, on Front Street, built by the Hudson Bay Company in 1853 to protect settlers from attack. Today it serves as a landmark, guarded by two of its original cannons.

Nanaimo is also famous for its chocolate bars. The bars have rich layers of chocolate on top, butter and icing sugar in the centre, and a mixture of graham crackers and coconut and more chocolate on the bottom.

Although several typical restaurants such as The Bluenose Chowder House, The Grotto and the Lighthouse Bistro specialise in local seafood, the Mexican food at Gina's is more fun. Perched on a cliff-top across from the law courts, this cosy little restaurant is friendly, prices are reasonable, the clientele interesting and the sunset views superb. Nanaimo claims more retail space per head than any other place in North America, so shoppers can have lots of fun.

Bathtub racing, a sport for the brave

BC's Bird Life

Both ornithologists and amateur naturalists love BC birdwatching, one of the fastest-growing recreational activities in the province. BC is home to some 400 species of birds, representing more than 80 per cent of all the species found in Canada. Birds are not only much less elusive than other wild creatures in BC, but also offer cheery songs without discrimination to both downtown city dwellers and adventurers on remote mountain trails.

The easily accessible Lower Mainland region is home to numerous species of birds, while others winter here to escape the northern Arctic winds and snows, and still others stop to feed and rest during annual migrations south and north.

In Vancouver, some elderly West End residents make a weekly ritual of greeting and feeding the ducks and swans around Lost Lagoon, on the fringe of Stanley Park. Park traffic sometimes stops to allow a gaggle of Canada geese to cross the road. At the rocky cliffs near Siwash Rock, cormorants, gulls and guillemots make their nests, and within the forest bald eagles are frequently seen perched on tall old trees.

Kingfishers and great blue herons are often seen hunting at Coal Harbour, Vancouver Island, along with loons, whose lonesome yodel symbolises the solitude of the Canadian wilderness.

Iona Island, in Richmond, is a good place to observe grebes, ducks, hawks, owls and passerines, while Pitt Meadows, in the Fraser Valley, is home to green herons, ducks, sandhill cranes, hawks and owls. But the best place for birdwatching is probably the Reifel Bird Sanctuary, located on the swampy, salty delta of the Fraser River. This area is home to Canada's largest concentration of waterfowl, including about 40,000 snow geese. The birds are best seen here from September to May.

Bird Alert (tel: 737–9910) provides details of rare and unusual birds recently sighted in the Greater Vancouver area.

The magnificent head of a golden eagle

Canada geese in flight at sunset

An elegant blue heron at rest

Wild geese beachcombing at Lund on the Sunshine Coast

Parksville

Nowhere in Canada does the ocean wash the shoreline so gently as it does along the popular sunny and sheltered bay at Parksville, the hub of Vancouver Island's east coast 'Beach Country'. Today, about 45,000 people live in the triangle formed by Parksville and nearby Qualicum Beach and Coombs.

When Captain Vancouver explored the area two centuries ago, only Coast Salish Indians were living here. First settled in 1870, Parksville prospered steadily for many years with an economy based on forestry, tourism and farming. But in recent years development has been more spectacular, with large numbers of Canadians moving in to settle and to spend vacations enjoying the area's special attractions.

Beaches and sandcastles

The waters of the Strait of Georgia flow in regularly twice a day along this coast. But whether the tide is in or out, there is ample space on the beach for a family outing or a solitary stroll.

Low tide leaves great expanses of hard clean sand several hundred metres wide. This is the time when beachcombers come to hunt for oysters and dig for clams, local residents walk their dogs, and visitors and their children wade in the shallow pools, fly kites and build sandcastles.

The week-long Sandcastle Contest every mid-July attracts master-builders from around the world, and they have to work quickly to complete their creations in the damp sand while the tide is out. Another competition is held specially for the children.

At high tide, the hot summer sand warms the incoming water to a comfortable swimming temperature. Parksville beach claims the warmest outdoor swimming conditions in the province, with summer temperatures averaging 21°C. The shallow water provides an ideal waterpark where youngsters may safely swim, splash about and ride dinghies and inner tubes.

The beach is probably at its most memorable in the early morning, when the loons are calling, the seals are barking and, across the water, the distant, deep mauve mountains are emerging against the orange sky.

South of Parksville, more than 2km of sandy shore also beckon at Rathtrevor Beach Provincial Park, one of the most popular family camping spots on Vancouver Island.

There are also 4km of hiking trails frequented by deer and rabbits, dozens of picnic tables and barbecue pits, children's play areas, a nature house, an amphitheatre and, in summer, nature interpretative programmes.

Special area attractions

As a change from the beach, Paradise Adventure Golf, centrally located in Parksville, also offers fun for the whole family. The two 18-hole miniature courses have a fantasy setting, with a pirate galleon, Victorian mansion, watermill, lighthouse and bright floral displays.

For further information on the Parksville-Qualicum Beach-Coombs area contact the Parksville & District Chamber of Commerce, PO Box 99, Parksville, BC VOR 2SO. The tourism information office is about 3km south of Parksville (tel: 248–3613).

For history lovers, Craig Heritage Park and Museum, 3km south of town, recalls the past with the 1912 Knox Church, the century-old French Creek post office, the McMillan loghouse, the Montrose school, a World War II fire station, and collections of late 19th-century clothing, old logging and farming equipment, and early photographs of the area.

The Parksville coast area is especially rewarding for birdwatchers, with its abundance of bald eagles, blue herons, loons, harlequin ducks and trumpeter swans.

Of the 57 species found here, 19 are on the North American birdwatchers' list of most keenly sought birds. One of these is the Brent goose, about 20,000 of which stop here during March and April to feed on the Pacific herring which spawns offshore, on the way to their Alaska nesting grounds. The event is celebrated every April during Parksville's Brent Festival.

A mini-golf fantasyland at Parksville, complete with watermill, offers fun for all the family in a delightful setting

The area is also a haven for anglers who come from far and wide to fish the waters.

Places to eat and stay

Accommodation for visitors in the Parksville-Qualicum Beach–Coombs area includes 1,500 hotel and motel units ranging from rustic cabins to modern condominiums and luxury beach resorts, with an additional 2,000 camping and recreational vehicle (RV) sites.

A range of fast-food and family eating places can be found along the Island Highway. There are also more elegant gourmet restaurants, including the picturesque historic MacLure House, once a private, Scottish-style manor house and now partly used as a small guesthouse.

QUALICUM BEACH

Qualicum Beach, a mecca for outdoor-lovers and fishing enthusiasts, recently celebrated 50 years as a town. The Old School House, affectionately known as TOSH, is about 80 years old and was renovated in the mid-1980s to house an art gallery with changing exhibits and eight studios with big viewing windows, so that visitors can watch resident artists at work.

Only slightly younger than TOSH is the Sunset Inn, on Memorial Avenue, which looks out to the golf course and the Strait of Georgia. The inn was originally built in 1919, and there are plans to rejuvenate it and bring back the past.

Numerous companies scattered along the coast offer charters of both power-

Many species of exotic butterflies are on view at Butterfly World near Coombs

boats and sailing-boats, large and small. Contact the French Creek Charter Boat Association *(tel: 248–3437)* for details. Travellers can launch their own boats at the Schooner Cove Resort, Beachcomber Marina, French Creek Marina, Qualicum Beach Marina, Bowser Bill's, La Bella Vista, Costa Lotta Campground or at Ship and Shore Marine.

Anglers flock to this area for the fighting coho, halibut and cod in the saltchuck around several offshore islands, and for the trout and steelhead in mountain streams and in the Big Qualicum, Little Qualicum and Englishman rivers.

Good golf courses in the neighbourhood include the Fairwinds (18 holes) on the Nanoose Peninsula, the Eagles Crest (18 holes) just south of Qualicum Beach, the Qualicum Beach Memorial (nine holes) on Crescent Road, and the Morningstar (18 holes) near the French Creek Marina.

COOMBS

A 10-minute drive inland from Qualicum Beach, following Highway 4 to Port Alberni and Long Beach, is the tiny town of Coombs, instantly identifiable in summer by the goats grazing on the grass roof of the roadside Old Country Market. The surrounding cluster of shops sells everything from candied apples and antler carvings to sportswear. The Bluegrass Festival and Old Time Fiddlers' Contest held every summer attract country and western fans from all over the continent – probably a far cry from the demure, God-fearing colony intended when Salvation Army Commissioner Coombs led a dozen English families here in 1910 to settle the area.

Nearby Butterfly World houses

hundreds of exotic butterflies, representing 70 species, flying free in an enclosed tropical garden. Visitors can watch butterflies emerging from cocoons, flying, courting, sipping nectar, laying eggs or simply basking in the sunlight. Be sure to brush any butterflies off your shoulders before you leave.

A few kilometres further along the highway westward, Hillier's Sausage Factory is an essential stop for campers and almost anyone else, since the European-style smoked meats made here are among the best in Canada. It is also worth the short bumpy ride from Coombs to Zipper-Mouth Rock Smoked Seafoods, which sells wonderful ready-to-travel prawns, oysters, smoked salmon and salmon pâté processed and packaged by a former commercial fisherman.

It is wise to phone ahead of a visit

Ancient stands of lofty Douglas firs survive in Cathedral Grove on Highway 4

(tel: 248–2079).

Two provincial parks where outdoor-lovers can walk, fish, swim, picnic or camp are also accessible from Coombs via Highway 4. East of town, and some 16km south of the highway, is Englishman River Falls Park, with its impressive waterfall, gorges and pools set in forests of cedar, hemlock and fir trees. Further west, on the way to Port Alberni, is Little Qualicum Falls with superb cataracts, pools and rocky chasms below Cameron Lake.

CATHEDRAL GROVE
About half-way along Highway 4 between Parksville and Port Alberni, stands Cathedral Grove, in McMillan Park. Well-marked wilderness trails, carpeted with coniferous needles and cedar chips, meander through lush ferns, hemlocks, cedars and a grove of 800-year-old Douglas fir trees, which survived a forest fire 300 years ago. The largest tree measures 3m in diameter and 9m in circumference, and stands 75m tall. Interpretative signs explain the woodland cycle of growth and decay. Little wonder this is called Cathedral Grove, for the elegant moss-draped trees create a sanctuary as awe-inspiring as any ancient religious building in Europe.

Port Alberni

*P*ort Alberni, a town of some 20,000 people, is the gateway to Vancouver Island's spectacular west coast and Pacific Rim National Park. About a three-hour drive from Victoria, it lies at the head of the long saltwater Alberni Inlet, midway along scenic Highway 4, which crosses the island's rugged interior. Named after the Spanish explorer Pedro Alberni, who passed through the area two centuries ago, the town sprawls around the lumberyards and mills of the MacMillan Bloedel timber company.

As the 'Salmon Capital of the World', Port Alberni is also a major fishing port, landing 20 per cent of BC's annual salmon catch from the 300 commercial fishing boats operating out of its harbour. Keen anglers flock here year-round to fish the salmon-rich waters of Alberni Inlet and nearby Barkley Sound. The most experienced especially enjoy Labour Day weekend here, when they compete in contests for more than $50,000 in prizes during the annual Salmon Festival. They also take part, along with well-known ice-hockey

Port Alberni – a town built on forestry

players, in the National Hockey League Celebrity Salmon Derby every year in August.

These competitions draw crowds to Alberni Harbour Quay, where the Clock Tower provides a panoramic view for miles around. Apart from the gift shops, art galleries, restaurants, and boat companies offering cruises and fishing charters, the lively quayside offers live outdoor entertainment and rides on the little 'Two Spot' steam engine. Also at the quay is the MacMillan Bloedel Forestry Information Centre, which provides a fascinating insight into the town's timber industry.

Port Alberni is a good base for various outdoor activities in the area. Nearby Mount Arrowsmith (1,800m), which is snow-capped for most of the year, has a number of forest trails which are suitable for hiking in summer or skiing in winter. A half-hour drive south of town along a rough logging road is China Creek, a popular spot for windsurfers where skill-testing regattas are held every summer.

SPROAT LAKE

Only a 15-minute drive west out of Port Alberni via Highway 4, the community of Sproat Lake borders the vast freshwater lake and provincial park of the same name. This is the home base of the Martin Mars water-bombers, the largest firefighting aircraft in the world, with tail-wing tips standing almost five storeys high. As they take off, these mammoth planes scoop up water from the lake to fight forest fires. Visitors are sometimes admitted to their land base, about a 10-minute walk east from the rustic Maples Resort on the north shore of the lake. But the planes are perhaps best seen from the deck of the Fish and Duck pub as they slowly become silhouettes against the setting sun.

One of the most dramatic rainforest walks in the world is the short and little-known, but marked, trail from the water-bomber base to Sproat Lake Park. From the campsites, picnic tables and boat-launching ramp in the park, it is another 10-minute walk east along the lakeshore to a floating dock from which some of the most interesting ancient petroglyphs on Vancouver Island can be viewed.

North of Sproat Lake, another intriguing place to visit is the Robertson Creek Hatchery on the Stamp River, where millions of chinook, coho and

Fishing – an ideal way to relax

steelhead are bred annually. Tours are available year-round, but the best time to visit is in September or October. During these months the mature salmon return upstream after four years at sea and leap up a series of fish ladders in Stamp Falls Park to spawn at their birthplace.

Sproat Lake is also a good jumping-off point for an exciting two- to four-day excursion that includes a canoe or water taxi ride along the entire length of nearby Great Central Lake, followed by a 16km hike along a trail to spectacular Della Falls. Plunging 444m in three magnificent cascades, the falls are among the highest in Canada.

PORT ALBERNI

The Lady Rose *ferry makes a brief stop on its journey down Alberni Inlet*

LADY ROSE

Gracious but hard-working, the MV *Lady Rose* is a sturdy 32m-long diesel packet, built in Glasgow in 1937, which has been ferrying freight and passengers for half a century. She is licensed to carry 100 passengers, and now offers visitors memorable sailing adventures.

At 8am, a shrill blast announces departure from the Port Alberni quay for the voyage westward down Alberni Inlet to the Pacific Ocean. Passengers take

A raft of loggers' hard work floats down towards the sawmills

breakfast or settle comfortably on the deck to enjoy the scenery.

Dark forests rise sharply from the edges of the broad fiord. The ship sails along at a steady 12 knots past China Creek and then ties up at the floating post office dock in Kildonan to unload mail and crates of goods. The next stops are at a couple of commercial fish farms, where groceries and pallets of fish food are delivered. Bald eagles circle overhead, hoping for left-overs. Then the *Lady Rose* sails on to several isolated logging camps and unloads mail and machinery parts.

Eventually the Broken Islands Group, in Barkley Sound, appear to the north. This cluster of about 100 small islands has several sheltered lagoons filled with sea birds and marine life that attract canoeists, kayakers and scuba divers. By noon the ship is docking at West Bamfield, where wooden boardwalks meander along the waterfront. As there is no road access here, water taxis cross the cove to East Bamfield, which is connected by a rough gravel logging road to Port Alberni. Accommodation is

A nautical view from aboard the Lady Rose

available for an overnight stay. Otherwise the stopover time here may be from 40 minutes to 1½ hours.

On alternate days in summer, the *Lady Rose* travels through the Broken Islands Group, stopping at Gibraltar Island or the Sechart Whaling Station, to drop off and pick up wilderness lovers laden with backpacks and other sporting equipment. She then stops for about an

IF YOU GO

Pack sun lotion, a warm sweater and a raincoat or windcheater, and wear sensible shoes. The weather in Alberni Inlet may vary from hot sunshine to heavy rain and strong winds. Bring a camera and binoculars for watching birds and possibly seals and grey whales. Canoes and single and double kayaks, to enjoy the raw natural beauty of the Broken Islands, can be hired on a daily or weekly basis.

Remember that the MV *Lady Rose* is a working vessel, so dress accordingly. For reservations and further information, call toll free 1–800–663–7192 from April to September; the rest of the year call 723–8313.

hour at the fishing village of Ucluelet before heading back up Alberni Inlet. The arrival back at Port Alberni is usually between 5.30pm and 6.30pm.

The Grenville Channel, Alberni Inlet

BC's Lumber Industry

Unloading timber from
a floating carrier at
Vancouver Island

BC's luxuriant forests, a
major economic resource
for the province and
for Canada

Log booms on
the Fraser River awaiting
transportation by rail to the mills

The Pacific Northwest rainforests, among the most luxuriant in the world, still contain ancient trees more than 1,000 years old. More than half of BC is covered in forest, most of it on Crown land.

The government grants tree-farming licences to logging companies, who are supposed to take care of the forest, clean up any waste and plant new trees. A dozen companies control more than 80 per cent of the provincial timber resources and more than 90 per cent of the pulp mills and plywood plants. Until the 1980s, only about one-third of the cleared land was being reforested. Fortunately that is now changing, as more people, not only in BC but around the world, are becoming increasingly aware of the necessity of preserving our planet and its resources. Public protests are forcing forestry companies to take better care of the forests, with selective cutting and more planting.

The traditional Paul Bunyan-style lumberjack in his long-sleeved checked shirt and heavy boots has disappeared. The axe has been replaced by the noisy roars of chain-saws, bulldozers, tree stumpers, hydraulic barkers, loaders, sorters and other machinery. In addition to loggers, the industry employs heavy-equipment operators, truck drivers, sawmill and pulp and paper-plant workers and tugboat captains, among others.

After the chain-saws fell the trees, the branches are removed, and cranes move the logs to the roadside, where loading machines stack the logs on to trucks. The logs are then carried to a dumping ground and are sorted, measured and bundled.

The biggest and best logs, such as the strong Douglas fir, go to plywood and other sawmills. Such smaller logs as western hemlock and balsam fir go to pulp and paper mills. Western red cedar, which is both weather- and rot-resistant, is often used for making roofing shakes and shingles.

Seasoning sawn timber in the open air

Pacific Rim National Park

*N*o trip to Vancouver Island is complete without a visit to wild and rugged Pacific Rim National Park on the western, rainy side of the island. Annual rainfall here averages 300cm, so before setting out call 726–4212 for the weather forecast. The park is divided into three units: from north to south, Long Beach, the Broken Islands Group, and the West Coast Trail.

LONG BEACH

Long Beach is accessible by car along a winding mountain highway from Port Alberni. Solitary walkers love this broad 11km-long stretch of surf-swept sand, rocky outcrops and tidal pools. Big drift-logs, bull kelp and brilliant sea anemones and starfish dot the sands, where lucky beachcombers can occasionally pick up glass fishing floats, watermarked like sterling silver to identify the villages in

Long Beach, remote and wild, is the most northerly unit of Pacific Rim Park

Japan from where they came. When summer surf is up at Incinerator Rock, it is fun to watch surfers catching the waves ashore.

The Wickaninnish Centre *(tel: 726–7333;* open daily, summer only) lends insight into the sometimes harsh haven that is the blue Pacific. Exhibits, murals, audio-visual presentations and other interpretative programmes explain the natural and human history of the region. The restaurant here is a good spot to admire the Pacific coast, especially on a rainy day.

The two towns nearby, Ucluelet and Tofino, offer a variety of restaurants and accommodation. Tofino, surrounded by water on three sides, has several craft shops and art galleries. The Blue Heron *(tel: 725–3227)* serves good seafood in an informal setting, and the Pacific Sands Beach Resort *(tel: 725–3322)* has 60 rooms with balconies overlooking Cox Bay.

THE WEST COAST TRAIL

Hardy hikers love the West Coast Trail, which meanders for 77km along an old telegraph route through wilderness rainforest, along sandstone cliffs and across slippery boardwalks in the southern part of Pacific Rim National Park. Once known as the graveyard of the Pacific for all the ships which sank off its shores, this coastline is rugged.

The hike, which takes about a week to complete, is not for the faint of heart. About a quarter of the hikers who set out do not manage to finish. But the challengers of this treacherous trail, accessible from mid-May to September only, are rewarded with the smell of the salty sea air; breathtaking views of undisturbed shoreline; sightings of and occasional pods of whales and pudgy sea lions, and such seabirds as pigeon guillemots, marbled murrelts and pelagic cormorants; such treasures as Tsusiat Falls, where several cascades have created super swimming holes near the shore; and a crackling campfire under the stars.

The trail runs from Port Renfrew to Bamfield, or vice versa.

Park – tel: 726–7721. Open: summer only; reservations required.
Pacific Sunset Nature Tours (tel: 437–3150) offer guided backpacking trips along the trail.

WHALE WATCHING

Every spring from mid-March to mid-April, Pacific Rim National Park becomes a popular place for whale watching. As their northbound migration reaches its peak, the 15m-long grey whales swim closer to shore, often pausing to play in the coves and fiord-like inlets along the coast. Although these leviathans of the deep are frequently sighted from rocky headlands along Long Beach, such charter boat companies as Jamie's Whaling Station in Tofino *(tel: 725–3919)*, organise excursions where the chances of sightings increase. Federal regulations stipulate that vessels must remain at least 46m from the whales, although some of the whales seem unaware of the regulations. A few greys stay in Clayoquot Sound for the summer and rejoin the parade back to Mexico in the autumn.

Fifty years ago there were an estimated 2,000 grey whales left in the world, but, thanks in part to the decline in whaling, there are now about 20,000. The Pacific Rim Whale Festival at Tofino and Ucluelet coincides with the peak of the north-ward migration and also includes crab races, a gumboot golf tourna-ment, concerts, exhibits and plays. The 'Whales in the Park' programmes include free guided whale-spotting hikes, lectures, films and displays.

Getting away from it all

Stretching in a great quadrangle between the 49th and 60th parallels, Canada's westernmost province brims with options for relaxation, recreation and adventure. Four times the size of Great Britain, BC's great outdoors covers 952,000sq km of mountains and valleys, rivers and lakes, rainforests and deserts, and coastlines and islands. The Pacific Ocean washes the shores of BC's main islands, Vancouver Island and the Haida Gwaii (Queen Charlottes). On Vancouver Island, Pacific Rim National Park lures whale watchers and other naturalists to wild beaches. Inland hikers explore the alpine meadows of Forbidden Plateau and Strathcona Provincial Park and the first-growth rainforest in the Carmanah Valley. Birdwatchers, kayakers and lovers of native Indian art and history like the Queen Charlottes for spotting such species as the rhinoceros auklet, paddling along calm inlets and studying moss-covered totems in abandoned villages.

A lake in the Okanagan Valley

East of Vancouver, the terrain opens into the Okanagan Valley, where waterslides and wineries flank dude ranches and bird sanctuaries. Further east, beyond the good hiking terrain of the Kootenays stand the majestic Rocky Mountains. A mere 100 million years old, the Rockies flank the Purcell Mountains, which have been around 15 times as long. The two became neighbours during the dinosaur era. The Burgess Shale site in Yoho National Park contains fossils from an ancient sea. More varieties of life are preserved here in fantastic detail than

exist in all our modern oceans.

The high interior plateau of the Cariboo Chilcotin attracts equestrians, some of whom head out from the Bracewells Circle X Ranch at Tatlayoko Lake to Potato Mountain to see grizzly bears and ice caves. Canadian River Expeditions offer a great 11-day circuit, which includes a boat cruise up the coast to Bute Inlet; a float-plane flight over the Homatho Icefield to turquoise Chilko Lake and a day of fishing and hiking; an exciting raft trip along the Chilko, Chilcotin and Fraser rivers to the town of Lillooet; and a scenic return to Vancouver aboard BC Rail.

North of the Cariboo Chilcotin stretches big-game country, where winter comes early. Stewart, Canada's most northerly ice-free port, has recorded as much as 27m of snowfall in one year. Winter lures visitors to explore the region by dog sled and skidoo and on nordic skis, while summer offers boating on Atlin Lake, rafting through icebergs on the great Tatshenshini River and game spotting in Spatsizi Plateau Wilderness Provincial Park.

BC's Beaches

*B*C's 12,000km coastline, dotted with 6,500 islands, boasts lots of beaches, most suitable for sunning, swimming and beachcombing in summer. Vancouver Island is surrounded by beaches, and the Sunshine Coast sports its share, too.

One of the province's most treasured beaches, like many precious things, is fairly remote. Travel to the end of Highway 101 to Lund, north of Powell River on the Sunshine Coast, and take the 15-minute water-taxi ride (tel: 483–9749) to Savary Island. This crescent-shaped gem is ringed with long, luscious beaches, reminiscent of the South Pacific. A warm current mingles with the tides to produce summer waters reaching 22°C. When Captain Vancouver landed here 200 years ago, after a long voyage through the South Seas, he admired this island for 'beauty such as we have seldom enjoyed'. The pace of life has not changed much since then. The three dozen permanent residents share Savary with many visitors, especially in summer. They come for the beautiful beaches, the warm waters and the many plants that normally grow much further south.

Near the government wharf, along 'Dough Row', windsurfers skim along with the breeze. Further away from human habitation, beachcombers find a variety of seashells, multi-coloured rocks and perfectly preserved sand dollars. Following the beaches around the island for about 30km is a full day's walk. The perfect way to end the day is with a bite to eat at the Mad Hatter Tea House, a 5-minute walk from the government wharf. A sign near by marks the trail to North America's largest arbutus tree. It takes four adults, arms stretched and touching at the fingertips, to circle the girth.

Visitors who want to linger longer will find two bed-and-breakfast places, but no campground. Overnighters who insist on sleeping on the beach are warned to watch for changing tides.

Fine secluded beaches can be found on boat trips along BC's Sunshine Coast

Boating

*M*ore than 250,000 BC households have boats. With so many waterways, boating seems as natural as driving. The choices are many and varied, ranging from a simple sunset dinner cruise around English Bay or a passive ride aboard a big BC ferry, to running the rapids of the mighty Fraser River or fishing offshore with whales, sea lions and cormorants for company.

DESOLATION SOUND
Lund, on the Sunshine Coast, and Campbell River, on eastern Vancouver Island, are good starting points for Desolation Sound, 32km north of Powell River. The largest of BC's 32 marine parks, Desolation Sound offers protected warm waters backed by coastal mountains. Native pictographs and coastal lakes make trips ashore interesting, and the waters provide fresh oysters and salmon for dinner.

PRINCESS LOUISA INLET
Jervis Inlet, further south on the Sunshine Coast, leads to Princess Louisa Inlet, one of the most scenic fiords in the world. Bordered by craggy granite cliffs streaked with waterfalls and capped with evergreens, the fiord is home to many sea mammals and birds. Erle Stanley Gardner said it best. 'There is no use in describing that inlet. Perhaps an atheist could view it and remain an atheist, but I doubt it.' At the head of the gorge is a marine park, crowned by the 40m-high Chatterbox Falls.

THE GULF ISLANDS
Sailing the sheltered waters of the Gulf Islands is also great fun. But watch for 'deadheads', mostly submerged waterlogged tree trunks which have escaped from log booms and could grind your vessel to an untimely halt. Some boat rental companies offer weekend flotilla charters, in which a group of boats sail in the company of a mother ship skippered by a certified instructor. The instructor does the navigating, thus enabling out-of-towners to explore unknown waters with ease. Courses are also offered in basic coastal cruising, coastal navigation, advanced sailing, celestial navigation and offshore sailing.

THE BOWRON LAKES CIRCUIT
The quietest and most relaxing boating adventure may be the Bowron Lakes circuit, named one of the top 10 canoe trips in the world by *Outside Magazine*. Deep in the heart of the Cariboo Mountains west of the Rockies, this rectangular chain of lakes and connecting waterways is set within a 121,600-hectare wilderness park. Along the 116km route, the placid blue waters reflect glacier-streaked mountains rising to 2,100m. The region is home to many birds and such other wildlife as moose, bear, lynx and beaver. Paddlers set off from Bowron Lake Lodge and Becker's Lodge, where a variety of canoes and camping gear can be rented. The circuit can be canoed any time from June to October, although June seems to be the best month for seeing both birds and other wildlife.

Lund provides access by boat to islands and inlets on the north Sunshine Coast

SHUSWAP LAKES

For a totally different boating holiday, head for the interior town of Sicamous, on the Trans-Canada Highway west of Revelstoke. Here visitors can rent a houseboat, complete with a hot tub on the deck, take the wheel and head out to tie up at one of 14 beaches on Shuswap Lake. The houseboats are simple to manoeuvre and great fun for families. Houseboaters can swim, fish and explore the area beneath the Shuswap Highlands from their floating home.

THE ATLIN LAKE WILDERNESS

For a boating adventure in the true north, head for Atlin, which lies near the BC/Yukon border. Atlin Lake, which is 100km long, is the place to be in mid-summer when the sun rises at 4.30am and sets at 11.15pm, leaving enough light to take midnight photos. Houseboaters, paddlers and sailors can also go ashore to hike, look for mountain goats, bathe in hot springs and admire alpine scenery.

The best way to get there is to fly to Whitehorse in the Yukon, and rent a car or catch the Atlin Express bus for the 3-hour ride south.

IF YOU GO

Request the BC Outdoor & Adventure Guide and Charter Boat Adventure brochures from Tourism BC or any BC Travel InfoCentre. Pathways Tours (tel: 263–1476) organises canoeing tours through the Bowron Lakes for novice paddlers.

Chilkoot Boat Tours in Whitehorse (tel: 668–7766) organises trips to and on Atlin Lake.

Running the Rapids

*S*uddenly a menacing sound rumbles ahead. There is no turning back now. 'Hang on tight!', shouts the boatman. The big rubber raft careens through the foaming rapids. Whitewater slams the pontoons, then gracefully sprays up and falls. And the raft plunges with the flow downstream to calmer waters.

This is rapid-running, but on such chauffeured expeditions, skilled rapid-runners man the oars. The rafts are not easy to capsize, but passengers wear life jackets, just in case. In rough water the raft may buck and leap like a Wild West bronco. River-running is not always a dry experience, so it is best to keep cameras in waterproof bags.

River-running is more than just navigating rivers. Most trips allow time for hikes ashore and a cooling swim in the river. On longer trips, the boatmen may become chefs and grill salmon steaks or hamburgers over an open fire, while the aroma of freshly brewed coffee fills the air. Often a happy evening can be spent around a campfire chatting with new-found friends, with time left over to gaze at the moon and stars before settling in for the night.

THE MIGHTY FRASER RIVER

Several powerful rivers surge through BC, carrying such Indian names as Chilko and Chehalis (meaning 'where the chest of a canoe grounds on a sandbar') and honouring such early explorers as Thomson and Fraser. But the Fraser River is the greatest of them all.

Rising as a trickle in the southeast corner of Mount Robson Provincial Park in the Rockies, the Fraser travels 1,280km southwest to empty into the Pacific. From Mount Robson, the river flows fast and pristine to Quesnel, where the blue waters turn turgid brown, due, at least in part, to chemical abuse by pulp mills. There are rapids at Scuzzy Rock, China Bar and at Hell's Gate, appropriately named, for here the mighty Fraser churns through a narrow, glacially carved 34m-wide gorge. As the raft runs from Boston Bar for 42km down to Yale, the boatman usually gives a running commentary on the mining history of the area.

For a more gentle trip, boaters start at Hope and wend their way past New Westminster to the Oak Street Bridge in Vancouver. This shows how the city is developing close to the river.

THE CRESTON VALLEY

Another gentle journey is the one- to three-day canoe trip through the Creston Valley. Paddlers start at the Canada/US border on Highway 21 and go north with the flow to Kootenay Lake. Protected marshlands make canoeing here quite safe.

More than 250 species of birds inhabit or visit the valley, and the area between Creston and Nelson is home to 140 pairs of osprey, one of the largest osprey nesting sites in the world.

Contact the Creston Valley Wildlife Management Centre *(tel: 428–3259)* for more canoeing information.

THE CHILKO RIVER

Another exciting rafting trip follows Chilko River, which falls into three sections. The run is a gentle one from Chilko Lake to Lava Canyon, where sets of grade-five rapids await the rafter. The last stretch runs from the Taseko River junction to the Chilcotin River junction.

Canadian River Expeditions
(tel: 738–4449)
Clearwater Expeditions
(tel: 579–8360)
Frontier River Adventures
(tel: 929–7612)
Hyak Wilderness Adventures
(tel: 734–8622)
Kumsheen Raft Adventures
(tel: 455–2296)

Running the whitewater rapids on the Chilliwack River east of Vancouver

SIMON FRASER

Simon Fraser was an American-born fur trader and explorer for the North West Company. He was also one of the great river-runners of the 19th century.

In 1808, against the advice of the native Indians, he led an expedition in birch-bark canoes down a river he believed to be the Columbia. He was mistaken, and that fast river of many rapids and deep gorges now bears his name. At Hell's Gate, Fraser wrote: 'It is so wild that I cannot find words to describe our situation at times... a desperate undertaking!'

His persistent and perilous journey changed the map of the continent.

Riding the Rails

*R*ailway buffs rate the daily five-hour BC Rail journey from Vancouver north to Lillooet one of the most scenic in the world. The train meanders along the north shore of English Bay through West Vancouver to Howe Sound. Here the tracks skirt the shore, while plumes of smoke from a pulp and paper mill on the fiord curl up into the rainforest mountains rising steeply on the other side. Railside towns, with such names as Squamish and Cheakamus (meaning 'those who fish with cedar rope nets'), recall the first inhabitants of this region.

The Royal Hudson steam train passes by stunning scenery on the way to Squamish

Beyond Whistler, where in winter skiers disembark to slalom down magnificent slopes, the train chugs through the verdant Pemberton Valley, farmed mostly to produce potatoes, and Mount Currie, a large First Nations reserve famous for its Victoria Day rodeo in May.

The town of D'Arcy, at the bottom end of Anderson Lake, introduces the most scenic section of the route. Around the lakes are scattered small communities, accessible only by rail or water. The cherry trees beside the track were planted by Japanese Canadians interned here during World War II. The surrounding Cayoosh Mountains sweep up to 2,700m to grassy meadows and grizzly bear country.

Each train is preceded by a little two-man speeder car that checks the line for landslides, and radios messages back to the engineer. When a town hangs out a tin flag, the train grinds to a halt, the conductor puts down the steps and passengers climb aboard.

Soon the lushness fades, as the dry belt emerges around Lillooet, a logging and mining centre with an Old West flavour. Miners register staked claims at the Court House, while the nearby Travel InfoCentre provides details on how visitors can pan for gold. Allow a night or two in Lillooet, or at the Tyax Mountain Lake Resort at Gold Bridge *(tel: 238–2221)*, before making the return journey to Vancouver.

Riding the Trails

*H*orseback riding is an easy and pleasant way to explore BC outdoors. Riding appeals to almost all ages: the views can be marvellous, the pace therapeutic, and the environmental impact minimal. Because the animals carry the gear, horseback holidays have extra appeal for families with young children who might find arduous hikes overwhelming. Most BC outfitters and dude ranchers use placid quarter horses and Arabian stock for trekking. They have comfortable gaits and respond to neck reining, which allows one hand free to hang on to the saddle horn.

In the Lower Mainland, latent cowpokes can canter in Golden Ears Park. Professional stables guide riders out of Maple Ridge for a day trek to Alouette Lake, where they can hitch their horses to a tree and go for a swim. Several hundred kilometres of trails in Manning Park are ideal for ambling through Canada's mountainous west. Late summer or autumn is a good season to ride, as the insects retreat and the autumn leaves turn bright red, rust and yellow. In mid-September at Manning, the alpine larch trees on Frosty Mountain turn a deep gold before dropping their deciduous needles.

North of Vancouver, at Williams Lake, riders can head west to Tatlayoko Lake in the Chilcotin for week-long journeys to see ice caves, fossil beds and meadows where grizzly bears forage in the Potato Mountain Coast Range. East of Williams Lake, riders can overnight at Helmcken Falls Lodge near Clearwater and ride lodge horses along the trails of Wells Gray Park.

For unusual trekking, try remote Mt Edziza Park, where the Tahtlan Indians introduce riders to moonscapes of cinder cones and mountains of shale, occasionally pockmarked by hungry

An exciting way to explore BC's great outdoors is on the back of a horse

grizzlies hunting gophers. Any saddle sores suffered during the long trek may be soothed by some hellebore root, which the guide boils up in an old tin can to ease the pain.

The Iron Horse

The history of the railway in Canada is the history of the development of this sprawling, rugged land. Where the iron horse ambled, settlers and prosperity usually followed. The first scheduled passenger train arrived in Vancouver in 1887. The arrival of the railway energised the economy of the Pacific Northwest, bringing large numbers of Canadians and Europeans. The population of Vancouver mushroomed from 900 to 8,000 people within five years, and the Canadian Pacific Railway became the city's largest employer.

The CPR built the first Hotel Vancouver, bought and sold land, operated sternwheelers on BC rivers and ran steamships across the Pacific Ocean. Freight trains running across the country encouraged the exploitation of natural resources. Such BC products as furs, coal, lumber, gold and fish suddenly had accessible markets.

The trans-continental train service has been curtailed in recent years, since cars and trucks, along with aircraft and helicopters, have dim-inished passenger demand. Most British Columbians now drive or fly to get from one place to another, but holidaymakers still love the romance and the rattle of the rails, the gentle pace, and the friend-liness of the conductors and other passengers from all over the world.

Yet the scenery remains the greatest attraction. Early CPR President Cornelius Van Horne commented back in 1895, 'Since we cannot export the scenery, we shall have to import the tourists'. Rail travellers love the stillness and splendour of the unfolding wilder-ness panorama of mountains, canyons, lakes, rivers, streams, forests and rolling ranchlands, and glimpses of such elusive wildlife as deer, elk, moose, bighorn sheep and bear. They love the dramatic spiral tunnel near Kicking Horse Pass. They love the geography lesson, with whistle stops at remote towns and villages bearing such intriguing names as Seton Portage, Boston Bar and Basque Junction. And they love the sense of pioneer adventure.

A mighty exhibit at the Forest Museum, Duncan, Vancouver Island

The CPR track winds its way along the Bow River

Getting up steam for Squamish

Provincial Parks

*T*here are more than 380 provincial parks in BC, encompassing glaciers, grasslands, rainforests, rivers and estuaries, lakes, dormant volcanoes, mountains, islands, fiords and beaches. There are 2,000km of hiking trails, and 90 parks with good canoeing and hiking, 240 with good fishing and 80 with boat launches. More than 12,000 campsites in 150 campgrounds are scattered throughout the parks. About 50 parks have interpretative programmes, so visitors can hear talks about flora and fauna and star-gaze with astronomers. Parks cover more than five per cent of BC, an area larger than the province of Nova Scotia.

Mount Robson Provincial Park, a favourite with many adventurers, contains the highest peak (3,954m) in the Canadian Rockies, the headwaters of the Fraser River and spectacular scenery, but has limited access. From June to September, visitors enjoy more than 50 species of alpine flowers, 170 species of birds (including golden eagles) and grizzly bears, caribou, mountain goats and hoary marmots. Pathway Tours *(tel: 263–1476)* runs heli-hikes into the park for people of all ages. The base camp, at 2,073m, nestles in a rain shadow surrounded by flowering meadows and snowy peaks.

Pure water flows in glacier-fed streams. Hikers bathe downstream in natural pools and waterfalls, and spend about six hours each day exploring. After an evening slide show in the main mess tent, the Northern Lights sometimes brighten the darkening sky.

Strathcona Park, BC's oldest park, boasts six of the seven highest peaks on Vancouver Island, along with the Comox Glacier, the island's last remaining ice-field, thus earning the nickname 'Little Switzerland' Although Strathcona is truly a wilderness park, day trippers take the half-hour drive west from Courtenay

in the Comox Valley in summer to enjoy the alpine flowers and hike the Forbidden Plateau.

Available accommodation includes campgrounds at Buttle Lake and Ralph River and the Strathcona Lodge *(tel: 286–8206)*, on the lake just outside the park. The lodge's superb outdoor education centre offers apprenticeships in wilderness leadership, rock climbing, mountaineering, whitewater canoeing, kayaking and photographing wildlife. Experienced hikers enjoy the Flower Ridge, Elk River and Marble Meadows trails radiating out from Buttle Lake, as well as the challenge of scaling the 2,200m Golden Hinde. Della Falls, the continent's highest at 460m, are located in the southern part of the park. Visitors take a water taxi from the Ark Resort *(tel: 723–2657)* near Port Alberni up Great Central Lake and then hike 16km to the falls.

Tweedsmuir Provincial Park is BC's largest. Many overseas visitors rent campers in Vancouver, drive north to Williams Lake on the Cariboo Highway (97) and then west on the Freedom Highway (20) to Bella Coola. This route runs through southern Tweedsmuir Park. Hair-raising switchbacks lead

Superb mountain scenery awaits visitors entering Mount Robson Park

down into the Atnarko River Valley, a good location for day hikes into the Rainbow Mountains.

The Dorsey family *(tel: 742–3251)* of Anahim Lake, guides in these parts for three generations, come highly recommended for week-long horseback outings during July and August. The Hunlen lakes area, which provides excellent canoeing, is where the pioneer settler Ralph Edwards helped save trumpeter swans from extinction during the 1950s. Ralph's son John runs the Hunlen Wilderness Camp.

Wells Gray Provincial Park, considered one of finest parks, is located just north of Clearwater, a five-hour drive north from Vancouver on Highway 5. The park offers great hiking in summer and hut-to-hut skiing in winter. Clearwater Lake is easily accessible and offers good beaches and good fishing. In winter the 142m Helmcken Falls freeze into a 20-storey-high ice cone, broader at the base than a football field. Helmcken Falls Lodge *(tel: 674–3657)*, was originally built as a hunting lodge at the entrance to the park. European visitors love it as a base for hiking, canoeing, backpacking, horseback riding, mountaineering, glacier exploration and fishing.

The Rockies

*T*his mountainous region of out-standing scenic splendour stretches northwest for 1,400km along the BC-Alberta border. It is bounded on the east by vast prairies and on the west by the Rocky Mountain Trench, one of the longest valleys in the world. Most of the Rocky Mountains are in Alberta. For much of their length, they form the Continental Divide separating Canada's east- and west-flowing rivers.

Mount Robson, the highest peak, shoots 4,000m skyward, while Mount Assiniboine, the Matterhorn of Canada, is a breathtaking 3,600m tusk of layered rock carved into a pyramid shape by glacial cirques.

The Rockies were created about 65 million years ago, when the land uplifted and broke along great fault lines, forcing the rock to fold and buckle. During the last Ice Age, about 12,000 years ago, glaciers completed the sculpting.

The Kootenay Indians have lived here for 10,000 years. As hunters and gatherers, they knew all the secret passes through the mountains. When the explorer and fur trader David Thompson eventually struggled through Howes Pass in 1807, the Kootenays nicknamed him 'Star Man'.

Although other explorers and traders, prospectors, missionaries and homesteaders (pioneer farmers) followed, few settled. The discovery of gold at Wild Horse Creek in 1863 brought a surge of 5,000 souls, but when the gold was gone only about 20 families remained. Two decades later the Northwest Mounted Police established a detachment here, headed by Superintendent Samuel Steele.

Modern travellers head here in passionate pursuit of the peaks and the outdoor action. The air is fresh, the

waters clear and the scenery awesome. From such guest ranches as Top of the World, Beaverfoot and Bull River, visitors can canter around the countryside all day and return to find freshly-caught rainbow trout sizzling on the grill. Others may prefer to hike over alpine meadows, play golf or paddle, sail, windsurf or water-ski on emerald lakes. Or they may savour the silvery cascades of Laughing Falls, or soak in warmer water at the Radium, Fairmont or Lussin hot springs.

Wildlife watchers, especially at dawn and dusk, may spot moose, deer, elk, mountain goat, bear, lynx, coyote and marmots. Winter resorts offer nordic and alpine skiing, while heli-skiing (heli-copter skiing) in the Bugaboo area is a thrill of a lifetime.

FORT STEELE
At this fine historic Heritage Town, the gold-mining past is vividly present in over 60 reconstructed buildings. Highlights include ice-cream making, stagecoach rides, re-created old newspapers, Victorian vaudeville at the Wildhorse Theatre, and workers costumed as blacksmiths, carpenters, quilters and weavers.
The town is 16km northeast of Cranbrook. Tel: 426–6923. Open: daily, dawn to dusk. Admission charge.

For further information, contact the Rocky Mountain Visitors Association at PO Box 10, Kimberley, BC V1A 2Y5. Tel: 427–4838.

Banff, in the Canadian Rockies, seen from a viewpoint on Sulphur Mountain

KIMBERLEY

Canada's highest city at 1,117m, Kimberley is nicknamed the 'Bavarian City of the Rockies'. The red-brick pedestrian Platzl holds the world's largest operating cuckoo clock. Bavarian-style buildings sport dark wood-panelling and floral decorations, and window-boxes filled with red geraniums. European delis and restaurants serve such German specialities as weisswurst, spetzle, and strudel. Kimberley has been a zinc-, silver- and lead-mining town since the 1890s. A 20-minute train ride carries visitors in an old mining car through a tunnel and over a trestle.

KOOTENAY NATIONAL PARK

Here a half-hour hike through moss-carpeted forest leads to the Paint Pots, ponds stained red, orange and yellow by iron oxide which the Kootenay Indians used for body and rock painting.
Located south of Yoho National Park. Open year-round.

YOHO NATIONAL PARK

With 28 peaks more than 3,000m high, all layered with rock, blue ice and snow, this park offers such varied sights as the Takakkaw Falls, the spiral railway tunnels leading up to Kicking Horse Pass, and the Burgess Shale fossil beds dating back 530 million years, which include petrified remains of 120 species.
Located just west of the Continental Divide and Banff National Park. Open year-round.

BANFF AND JASPER NATIONAL PARKS (ALBERTA)

Canada's oldest national park, Banff was established in 1885 after hot springs were seen gushing from the side of Sulphur Mountain. The main resort towns are Banff, named after Banffshire in Scotland, and Lake Louise, located at the Continental Divide.

Jasper National Park, the largest designated parkland in the Rocky Mountains, lies north of Banff and west of Edmonton. Scenic highlights include Mount Edith Cavell and Maligne Lake, a large and beautiful remnant left by a retreating glacier. The Columbia Icefield, a glacier that has not yet retreated, is about an hour's drive south.

Shopping

*W*estern Canadians have been shopping in Vancouver ever since the Oppenheimer brothers began outfitting prospectors and homesteaders more than a century ago.

Perhaps due in part to rainy weather, clusters, both small and large, of indoor shops attract the greatest number of browsers and buyers. Shopping malls seem to have replaced the village squares and fountains of yesteryear. Shopping has become more than just buying. It has become a pastime, a recreation, an entertainment, an education and sometimes a destination. Adolescents,

The flavour of the Orient at Granville Island's public market

adults and senior citizens hang around in malls to meet, watch passers-by and pass the time. Shopping is a socially acceptable solitary activity. Most stores are open from Monday to Saturday, 9.30am –5pm (extended on Thursday and Friday to 9pm) and Sunday noon–5pm.

Anything visitors might need is available, often for lower prices than in Europe. Downtown and suburban stores sell the latest European and Hong Kong formal and casual fashions, cheap and expensive souvenirs, work-clothes for

lumberjacks and fishermen, nautical needs, and do-it-yourself kits to build everything from armoires to automobiles.

Souvenirs to remind you of BC after you get home include such native-crafted items as masks, totems and other carvings in red and yellow cedar, soapstone, jade and argillite, along with woven baskets, paintings, delicate silver jewellery, moccasins and hand-knitted sweaters from the Cowichan Valley north of Victoria. Smoked salmon, vacuum-packed for travel, is sold at most souvenir shops and in supermarkets.

For the ultimate trendy and practical Canadian souvenir, go to Tilley Endurables at 1537 West Broadway, Vancouver, for a Tilley hat, which floats, ties on, repels rain, won't shrink, and comes with a lifetime guarantee and a four-page owner's manual.

MARKETS

Vancouver now enjoys half-a-dozen European-style markets, most of which have sprung up during the past decade. Most offer an array of fresh bread, pastries and pasta; local and exotic fruits, vegetables, flowers and other plants; fresh meats and seafood; fast-food stalls serving snacks from all over the world; luxurious restaurants within walking distance; free entertainment by musicians, jugglers and storytellers; complimentary parking; and shops selling designer kitchenware, local and imported wines, Canadian crafts and souvenirs and other goods.

BRIDGE POINT MARKET

This is a refreshing place to visit between flights at Vancouver Airport, a five-minute drive away. The market is landmarked by a modern 43m-high clock tower.

8811 River Road, Richmond. Tel: 273–8500. Open: Tuesday to Sunday 9am–6pm.

GRANVILLE ISLAND MARKET

This is the oldest of several waterfront markets and features a broad outdoor deck overlooking the bustle of marine activity in False Creek.

On Granville Island; accessible by AquaBus from the foot of Granville Street. Tel: 666–6655. Open: Tuesday to Sunday 9am–6pm.

LONSDALE QUAY MARKET

This market houses a wide selection of shops ranging from Harriet's House, which specialises in handmade Canadian quilts and toys to Out of Africa, with its array of musical instruments, crafts, artefacts, clothing and jewellery from Africa.

123 Carrie Cates Court, North Vancouver; accessible by SeaBus from downtown. Tel: 985–6261. Open: daily 9.30am–6.30pm; hours extended Friday to 9pm.

ROBSON MARKET

Upstairs here, artisan-vendors sell their wares around a cluster of cafés, backdropped by a spectacular 43m-long mural depicting life in the West End and overlooking colourful displays of produce below.

A 10-minute walk from city centre at 1610 Robson Street. Tel: 682–2733. Open: daily 9am–9pm.

WESTMINSTER QUAY MARKET

Getting here is half the fun, involving a spectacular 30-minute ride by SkyTrain from downtown. The market overlooks the Fraser River.

810 Quayside. Tel: 520–3881. Open: daily 9.30am–6.30pm.

Downtown Shopping

*T*he main shopping and browsing streets are Water Street in Gastown for Canadiana, Robson Street for clothes and cafés, Pender Street in Chinatown, and South Granville Street for art, antiques and carpets.

PACIFIC CENTRE MALL

This shopping area spreads over and under three downtown city blocks, where a three-storey waterfall, a glass rotunda and skylighted atrium attempt to bring the outdoors indoors.

Eaton's and The Bay (Hudson's Bay Company), both big department stores, offer good bargains during sales and guarantee satisfaction or money refunded. And there are 200 other small stores and services.

Universal Leather (near the Granville Street entrance) offers Canadian-made multi-coloured leather jackets, including the UN special, which flies the flags of many nations front and back.

The East Bay Science & Nature Company sells such interesting items as a terracotta sundial, a squirrel-proof seed dispenser for feeding birds, a leaf-collecting album for children, burnished wind chimes with a 345-year guarantee, and a quail call whistle.

The Music Box Company carries even hard-bitten adults back to the magic moments of childhood with hundreds of music boxes ranging from delicate carousels to handcrafted wooden boxes imported from Italy.

Godiva Chocolatier shows and sells tasty chocolates in shell shapes and prepares custom-tailored gift baskets while opera music plays in the background.

The Den for Men is a small shop chock-a-block with such gift items as a foot massager, an electronic putting partner and pocket-sized computer games.

At Georgia and Granville Streets. Tel: 688–7236. Open: Monday to Saturday 9.30am–5.30pm; extended on Thursday and Friday to 9pm; Sunday noon–5pm.

ROBSON STREET

This street, once reminiscent of parts of Europe but becoming more like Tokyo's Ginza district, is the most popular strolling street in Vancouver. Here people meet and greet, gaze at store

Fashionable Robson Street is Vancouver's most prestigious shopping thoroughfare

windows filled with clothes and curios from around the globe, and linger in the cafés and restaurants to watch the world go by.

On the south side of Robson Street between Seymour and Burrard streets is **Bobby Dazzler**, one of the most interesting stores in the area. Staff here do not bother browsers, intrigued by such innovative items as a Phantom electronic chess set, a levitating globe, top-of-the-line roller blades and kneepads, a safari hat with a mini-solar-powered fan, a VoicePrint phone and a collection of flower seeds inspired by the French artist Claude Monet's garden in Giverny, France.

The next block west on Robson, between Burrard and Thurlow streets, is lined with more than 40 shops specialising in shoes, clothing, flowers, souvenirs, foreign book exchange, jewellery, books, cutlery, satchels and lasers.

Even in a country like Canada, where land is plentiful, Robson Street property is too expensive to have people lingering long in cafés, so there are few pavement tables.

Starbuck's, which sells the best coffee in the city, has two cafés at Robson and Thurlow streets, but only three outdoor tables. This complicates life for some, as smoking is not permitted inside.

This same city block contains **London Drug**, with everything from video cameras to dog food, and the lowest prices in town. It is a good place to stock up on such sundries as toothpaste and shampoo.

SINCLAIR CENTRE

A few blocks north towards Canada Place, this restored historic building houses a small cluster of shops circling

Shoppers can browse in comfort in the huge downtown Pacific Centre Mall, a glittering indoor palace

an elegant skylit atrium, where musicians entertain and artists display their works. Favourite shops include **Leone's**, a galleria of exquisite European designer creations complete with espresso bar; **Gulliver's Travel Accessories**; **Cole's Books**, a post office, a dental surgery with a neon tooth in the window, and several fast-food outlets.

757 West Hastings Street. Tel: 666–4483. Open: Monday to Saturday 10am–5.30pm.

Prettily dressed dolls in a downtown shop window are sure to catch the eye

SUBURBAN SHOPPING

The latest sprawling suburbs of Vancouver are dotted with spacious malls, reflecting the latest trends in architecture, design and consumer goods. The modern Metrotown Centre, in Burnaby, has parking for 3,500 cars and is linked to the city centre by SkyTrain and hundreds of buses daily. The Oakridge Shopping Centre, at West 41st Avenue and Cambie streets, contains 150 stores, including **Woodward's** department store, **Rodier Paris, Abercrombie & Fitch, Edward Chapman, Ports, Bally Shoes, Bowrings of Newfoundland** and the **Salt Box**. An air of quiet sophistication prevails in this spacious, skylighted mall.

PARK ROYAL

This mall, opened more than 40 years ago as Canada's first major shopping centre, services the North Shore. Many shoppers who live near by are retired, so the mood is basically relaxed and unhurried.

The North Mall is anchored by **Woodward's** department store on the east end and by a **Safeway Supermarket** at the west, linked by two walkways lined with shops. Favourite shops include **Royal Seafoods** for fresh products of the Pacific; the **Royal Rug & Curio Shop** for traditional Chinese wedding baskets (the 'hope chests' of the East) and superb slippers at low prices; **Daniadown Quilts** for warm and lightweight German-style bed covers; and **Toys & Wheels** which has a great selection of jigsaw puzzles and cuddly teddy bears.

Other top shops include **Deeler Antiques** for splendid Tiffany lamps and grandfather clocks; **Marielle's** for stylish scarves and opera jackets; **Herzog's** for painted papier-mâché boxes from Kashmir and Rosenthal china (often less expensive than in Europe); and **Shirley K Maternity** for bold, blossoming fashions. A stop at **Gizella's** Swiss-style restaurant for an Emmenthal burger or sachertorte provides a pleasant pause to refresh and watch other shoppers wander past.

At the South Mall, **Eaton's** and **The Bay** (Hudson's Bay Company) department stores dominate. The Bay cafeteria, located inside the store, has good food, reasonable prices and panoramic windows looking out over English Bay and the Lions Gate Bridge. In the western atrium of the mall, a terrace café, near the open escalator and the glass elevator, offers a superb spectacle – a walk-on chess set with enormous pieces.

There are several interesting shops to see. **Peter Black & Sons** sells haggis and oatcakes. Next door, the **Gourmet Pasta Shop** stocks French cheeses, Italian pasta, olive oil and salami. The **Bombay Company** features a selection of small furniture, oak-framed flora and fauna prints, and large lacy bird cages. The **Coach House** displays such giftware as Italian and Canadian pottery, Inuit prints and silver-plated photo frames.

The bargain basket near the door of **Sweater Craft** is usually filled with warm cardigans and pullovers at reduced prices. At **The Zoo**, the theme is animals, stuffed, silk-screened and printed, and varying in price from a few to a few hundred dollars.

Marks & Spencer sells clothing and food items. The **BC Automobile Association** next door sells travel insurance, package tours, accommodation and airline tickets to both members and non-members.

Park Royal is just west of the north end of the Lions Gate Bridge, straddling Marine Drive. There is always ample parking, but it takes only 10 minutes on the Blue Bus to get here from Georgia Street downtown.

Tel: 922–3211. Open: Monday to Saturday 10am–6pm; hours extended on Thursday and Friday to 9pm, Sunday noon–5pm.

For shoes, the chic shops along Robson Street are the most tempting in town

OTHER SHOPPING HIGHLIGHTS

VICTORIA

Victoria has a variety of shops and galleries, many selling British china and woollens, antiques, Canadian native prints and carvings, and warm hand-knitted Cowichan sweaters. The **Northern Passage**, housed in an elegantly restored Victorian heritage building at 1020 Government Street *(tel: 381–3380)*, sells distinctly Canadian crafts and other items ranging from fine pottery and silver jewellery to fluffy little abstract sheep which play Brahms's *Lullaby* when patted on the back. **Munro's Book Store**, at 1108 Government Street *(tel: 382–2464)*, is renowned for its great selection of books, but is worth a visit if only to see the magnificent domed ceiling, stained-glass windows and wall hangings.

SHOPPING IN ALBERTA

The **Sport Tour** company organises shopping tours to West Edmonton Mall in Alberta, which is free of provincial sales tax. Prices start at about $500 per person, including airfare, transfers and two nights' accommodation.
Tel: 732–7622.

CROSS-BORDER SHOPPING

Ask most British Columbians the best place to shop and chances are they will direct you south of the border. More than 21 million shoppers pass through the five BC-US border stations between Boundary Bay and Abbotsford each year. Many go to the US for half an hour, just long enough to fill up the car with petrol, and to buy $20 worth of milk, butter,

Stylish elegance is the hallmark of many shops on Vancouver's Granville Street

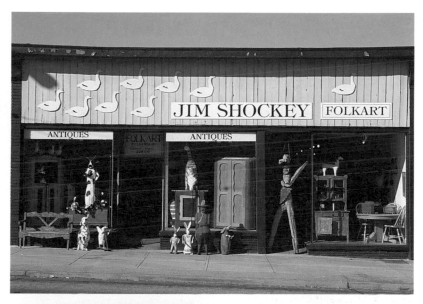

The art galleries on Granville Street are the places to go for fine paintings

Opportunities to hunt for treasures abound in BC's numerous antique stores

cheese and maybe a pack of cigarettes and a six-pack of beer. The prices are up to a third cheaper. Other people go to buy new tyres or for vehicle repairs with no goods and services tax.

Most Vancouverites drive just across the border to Blaine or Bellingham, or to Point Roberts, a tiny peninsula of American land near Tsawwassen,

accessible to other Americans only by driving through Canada. The vast parking lot at Bellingham's Bellis-Fair Mall, about an hour's drive south from Vancouver, is often filled with the motorhomes of Canadian shoppers staying the 48 hours required in order to bring in duty-free goods. A 10-minute drive south from Bellis-Fair, right beside the freeway, stands a cluster of retail shops sporting designer names at wholesale prices. Clothing is generally less expensive in the US than in Canada and the selection more varied.

European visitors usually have no problem with Canada customs upon returning from the US, as long as they can produce a return ticket to Europe, implying that goods purchased will not stay in Canada.

Entertainment

*F*ew people come to Vancouver for entertainment, except for the outdoor variety so bountifully offered by Mother Nature. But Vancouver is a quietly vibrant city and does offer such various indoor options as ballet, opera, classical music, rock, jazz, theatre and cinema, featuring respectable local, national and international talent.

Street entertainers add a touch of fun to the scene all over Vancouver

The daily newspapers, the *Vancouver Sun* and *The Province*, along with the free weeklies, *The West Ender* and the *Georgia Strait*, contain advertising and editorial reviews of current entertainment. *WHERE Vancouver*, a compact monthly magazine free in most hotels, provides details of musical and theatrical performances, along with listings of cabarets, clubs and jazz gigs.

The **Arts Hotline** *(tel: 684–ARTS)* provides information on the performing arts, and the **Coastal Jazz and Blues Society** *(tel: 682–0706)* offers information on current and future jazz events.

For recorded information on current movies and cinema locations, call **Cineplex Odeon** *(tel: 687–1515)*, **Famous Players** *(tel: 681–4255)* or the individual independent cinemas.

All kinds of street entertainers are scattered throughout the city, but especially on Robson Street. However, the best shows usually materialise on Granville Island on sunny Sunday afternoons. Here, on the wooden deck in front of the market overlooking False Creek, jugglers, clowns, storytellers, mime artists, guitarists and other musicians politely compete for attention.

TICKETS

Ticketmaster *(tel: 280–4444)*, which has outlets in Eaton's department stores and at information counters in major malls throughout the city, sells tickets for cultural and sporting events. Ticketmaster has special lines for arts events *(tel: 280–3311)* and spectator sports *(tel: 280–4400)*.

BALLET, OPERA AND CLASSICAL MUSIC

Ballet BC *(tel: 669–5954)*, Canada's Royal Winnipeg Ballet and such well-known visiting dance companies as the Kiev Ballet perform at the 2,800-seat **Queen Elizabeth Theatre**, at 630 Hamilton Street.

Also at the Queen Elizabeth, the Vancouver Opera *(tel: 682–2871)* and visiting opera companies present 20th-century productions and such timeless masterpieces as *The Marriage of Figaro* and *Don Pasquale*.

At the adjacent Vancouver Playhouse, the **Festival Concert Society** *(tel: 736–3737)* features reasonably priced Sunday Coffee Concerts for the whole family from September to June. The entertainment varies from classical music to folk dancing. In-house baby-sitting is available for a minimum charge.

Many musical events are also held at the gracious and elegant **Orpheum**, located at 884 Granville Street, Smithe *(tel: 665–3035)*. The Orpheum is the

Musicians and other entertainers often perform for crowds on Granville Island

home of the **Vancouver Symphony** *(tel: 876–3434)*, which also performs at various other Lower Mainland venues and at several outdoor locations during the summer.

The **Ramcoff Concert Society** (tel: 986–6838), BC's only classical chamber music society run by professional musicians, offers noon concerts at a number of public sites. Free lunchtime concerts are often held on the plaza in Robson Square during July and August. Other musical events take place at the **Vancouver East Cultural Centre** at 1895 Venables Street *(tel: 254–9578)*.

Headphones for people with hearing disabilities are available at the Queen Elizabeth Theatre, the Vancouver Playhouse and the Orpheum. All these places are wheelchair accessible.

JAZZ

There are many good jazz artists and good places to enjoy them in Vancouver. At the **Alma Street Café**, 2505 Alma Street *(tel: 222–2244)*, the music plays from 7.30pm Wednesday to Saturday. Both food and service are excellent, and reservations are advised. The **Café Django**, at 1184 Davie Street *(tel: 689–1184)*, features jazz Thursday to Sunday from 8.30pm. The restaurant has an interesting menu and a balcony overlooking English Bay. Reservations are advised. At **Carnegie's Bar and Grill**, 1619 West Broadway *(tel: 733–4141)*, mainstream jazz pianist Bob Murphy and various guests entertain.

The **Glass Slipper**, at 185 East Eleventh Avenue *(tel: 877–0066)*, is a co-operative rehearsal and performance hall for good local and imported talent. It is open from Wednesday to Sunday 9pm–1am. **Chardonnay's**, at 808 West Hastings *(tel: 684–1511)*, has jazz

Sometimes a little jazz livens up the lunch break for Vancouver city workers

Thursday to Saturday 9pm–1am. The **Rattlesnake Grill**, at 2340 West Fourth Avenue *(tel: 733–2911)*, offers blues every evening from 8pm, while diners savour such delicacies as grilled diamond-back rattlesnake in a comfortable southwestern adobe setting. Reservations are recommended. The **Troller Pub**, at 6422 Bay Street in Horseshoe Bay *(tel: 921–7616)*, is popular for live local jazz early Saturday evening.

The annual du Maurier Jazz Festival is held in late June at various venues throughout Vancouver. For more information, call the **Jazz Hotline** *(tel: 682–0706)*.

ROCK AND CONTEMPORARY MUSIC

Big Canadian and international names

entertain regularly at **BC Place Stadium**, which seats 60,000 people, and the **Pacific Coliseum** on the Pacific National Exhibition grounds. Smaller places to hear good rock and budding local talent include the **Commodore Ballroom**, at 870 Granville Street *(tel: 681–7838)*, and 86 **Street Music Hall**, at 750 Pacific Boulevard *(tel: 683–8687)*.

THEATRE

The **Arts Club Theatre** *(tel: 687–5315)* offers the best in live theatre, ranging from classical Shakespeare to popular drama and contemporary works created by local playwrights. Programmes are presented year-round at the **Mainstage** and **Revue** theatres on Granville Island. Also on Granville Island, the **Waterfront Theatre** *(tel: 685–6217)* stages outstanding Canadian plays, while the adjacent Carousel Theatre entertains youngsters. The **Vancouver Playhouse** *(tel: 872–6622)*, housed in the same building as the Queen Elizabeth Theatre at 630 Hamilton Street downtown, stages six full-scale productions each season, including classic and contemporary drama, comedy, musicals and at least one Canadian play.

Theatre Under The Stars *(tel: 687–0174)* has been putting on Broadway-style musicals for half a century at the Malkin Bowl bandstand outdoors in Stanley Park. The show continues from mid-July to mid-August, weather permitting. It's especially fun with a picnic under a full moon. The **Vancouver East Cultural Centre**, at 1895 Venables Street *(tel: 254–9578)*, seems to specialise in avant-garde theatre, complemented by visual art exhibitions.

The **Theatre Sports League** presents hilarious improvisations, often involving the audience, at the Back Alley Theatre, 751 Thurlow Street *(tel: 688–7013)*, from Monday to Saturday from 8pm. At the **Punchlines Comedy Club**, 15 Water Street *(tel: 684–3015)*, stand-up comics from all over the continent entertain from Tuesday to Saturday from 9pm. **Yuk Yuk's**, at 750 Pacific Boulevard *(tel: 687–5233)*, also specialises in stand-up comedy.

BARD ON THE BEACH

The Bard on the Beach Theatre Society *(tel: 325–5955)* presents Shakespearean favourites in an open-ended candy-striped tent seating 300 people in Vanier Park adjacent to the Planetarium, on evenings in July and August. The setting is spectacular, as the stage has a backdrop of the North Shore mountains and sky coloured by the setting sun. Prices are reasonable, and reservations are recommended.

The Kitsilano Showboat provides outdoor entertainment overlooking English Bay

CINEMA

Vancouver has dozens of cinemas showing the latest feature films. Most are to be found downtown on the Granville Street Mall. There are also several small cinemas in the Royal Centre Mall under the Hyatt Regency Hotel.

The **Pacific Cinémathèque**, at 1131 Howe Street *(tel: 688–8202)*, is a non-profit educational society dedicated to the enjoyment and study of film. Emphasis is on non-commercial classics such as *Bagdad Café* and Derek Jarman's *The Garden*.

The **Ridge**, at 3131 Arbutus Street *(tel: 738–6311)*, also features the classical and off-beat, serves delicious carrot cake and cappuccino, and has a crying room for kiddies.

Closer to downtown, the **Starlight Cinema**, at 935 Denman *(tel: 689–0096)*, also screens classical and unusual films.

The annual **Vancouver Film Festival** *(tel: 685–0260)*, which takes place in early October, offers the best in current cinema from around the world. Hotel room television sets offer entertainment from more than a dozen channels, as well as a selection of pay-TV films.

If you have a VCR hundreds of video shops scattered throughout the city rent thousands of videos (mostly VHS), ranging from children's comedies to heavy drama.

CASINOS

Gambling is highly regulated in Canada. Two of the major casinos, the Great **Canadian Casino** *(tel: 291–WINS)* and the **Royal Diamond Casino** *(tel: 685–2340)*, abide by this. Dice are not permitted, so games are limited to roulette, blackjack and sic bo. Non-alcoholic beverages and snacks are available. Fifty per cent of the proceeds go to local charities. Both casinos are open seven nights a week 6pm–2am. The Royal Diamond Casino is at 1195 Richards Street. The Great Canadian Casino has four locations in the Lower Mainland. The closest one to downtown is in the Holiday Inn at 711 West Broadway.

DISCOS AND CLUBS

Club Mardi Gras

This club boasts state-of-the-art sound and light shows, with top hits of the last four decades, a wine bar and a Cajun kitchen.
1015 Burrard Street. Tel: 687–0575.

Club Soda

This club features theatre seating, with live bands and videos and a good dance floor.
1055 Homer Street. Tel: 681–8202.

Kits on Broadway

A lively DJ who favours mainstream rock 'n' roll keeps this cabaret swinging.
1424 West Broadway. Tel. 736–5811.

Notorious Nite Club

A classic rock 'n' roll party room for pool, darts, pinball and dancing.
364 Water Street. Tel: 684–1968.

Richards on Richards

At this club there are live bands for dancing to the tunes of the Top 40, with recorded music between sets, and video backdrops. Bar snacks are served, but no meals.
1036 Richards Street. Tel: 687–6794.

Town Pump

This club is a favourite with locals, who

like the local and imported bands, the extensive selection of beer and videos and the full dinner menu.
66 Water Street. Tel: 683–6695.

DINNER PLUS

Blarney Stone
This lively Gastown restaurant features Irish and contemporary entertainment, starting nightly at 9pm.
216 Carrall Street. Tel: 687–4322.

La Quena Coffee House
Reasonably priced Latin-American food is served here all day. Evening entertainment ranges from videos to such great imported music groups as Ancient Cultures and speeches on political and community issues.
1111 Commercial Drive. Tel: 251–6626.

Mulvaney's
The tasty Cajun cuisine and the Deep South setting are complemented

Live entertainment at the Plaza of Nations, site of the 1986 World's Fair

nightly between 9pm and 1am by DJ music for dancing.
Granville Island. Tel: 685–6571.

Soft Rock Café
This restaurant serves a set meal to the sounds of the Top 40 played by live bands. The meal is rarely the highlight of the evening.
1925 West Fourth Avenue. Tel: 736–8480.

The Roof
This restaurant serves fine food to the sound of local musicians playing swing, big band, jazz and romantic Julio Iglesias-style music from Tuesday to Saturday from 8.30pm to midnight. The central dance floor is great for an old-fashioned waltz.
Under the copper roof of the Hotel Vancouver. Tel. 684–3131.

Children

*V*ancouver offers an abundance of attractions to entertain and educate youngsters. Some activities mentioned here are described in more detail in other parts of this book. For more suggestions, check Daniel Wood's book, *Kids! Kids! Kids!* in Vancouver and the Friday 'Family Fun' column in the *Vancouver Sun*.

DOWNTOWN

The **OMNIMAX** Theatre, at Canada Place *(tel: 682–IMAX)*, is a 400-seat cinema with a five-storey-high wrap-around screen and superb sound facilities. Five different delightful short films offering scenic spectacles, outdoor adventure and even space travel are shown daily.

Science World, at 1445 Quebec Street *(tel: 687–7832)*, provides enough hands-on educational enjoyment for a whole day, and has a cafeteria on site for lunch. It is an ideal place to take children on a rainy day. The OMNIMAX cinema presents six shows daily. See page 75.

Stanley Park is a wonderful playground for both young and old. While anyone young at heart enjoys the playful otters and monkeys, children especially love the Petting Zoo *(tel: 681–1141)* and the Miniature Railway *(open: 11am–4pm daily)*, which rambles through a mini-wilderness and offers views of bighorn sheep, kangaroos, peacocks and wolves.

At the Aquarium *(tel: 685–3364)*, kids enjoy touching the sea cucumbers, anemones, starfish and chitons (molluscs). They also love watching the killer whales in playful mood as they socialise, swim and splash.

For more water fun, there is the saltwater swimming pool – an enjoyable

and safe option, which is supervised by lifeguards at Second Beach; and then there are the water water parks on the Seawall near Lumberman's Arch and beside the fire engine playground near Pacific Avenue. Kids can burn up extra energy by cycling around the scenic 10km Seawall.

Bicycle rentals are available near the Georgia Street entrance to the park.

GRANVILLE ISLAND

The best way to plan a visit to Granville Island is to stop at the Information Centre at 1592 Johnston Street *(tel: 666–5784)*, open daily 9am–6pm, to get maps and brochures. Then head for the Public Market, open daily 9am–6pm except Monday, to feast on anything from fresh fruit to fudge, on the theory that kids are more contented with full tummies. In good weather, jugglers, musicians and colourful clowns entertain on the wooden deck in front, beside False Creek. While strolling through nearby streets, children can get a glimpse of crafts in the making by peering through the windows to watch weavers, printmakers, glassblowers and sculptors at work.

The **Kids Only Market**, at 1496 Cartwright Street *(tel: 689–8447)*, houses two dozen shops and other diversions. It is open daily 10am–6pm from June to

August, but closed Monday the rest of the year. On the south side outside is a Playcare Centre for youngsters aged three to five.

Weary parents can revive with a cappuccino at Isadora's, while children shower each other with big fire hoses attached to revolving fire hydrants at the supervised summertime **Water Park** in front. The restaurant is reasonably priced and has a small children's play area inside for rainy days.

The **Arts Umbrella**, at 1268 Cartwright Street *(tel: 681–5268)*, runs two-week day and half-day camps in summer for kids up to the age of 18 (9am–3.30pm, with shorter days for pre-school children). Classes include sculpture, dance, drama, painting, drawing and wood-carving. Reservations are advised.

Families can share outdoor fun with rental kayaks from **Ecomarine**, at 1668 Duranleau Street *(tel: 689–7575)*, and paddle around False Creek.

UNIVERSITY OF BRITISH COLUMBIA

The **Museum of Anthropology** *(tel: 822–3825)* lets children beat hanging drums and pull out dozens of drawers to examine native Indian toys, jewellery and clothing. Children enjoy feeding the fish at the Nitobe Japanese Gardens, watching cows being milked at the UBC Dairy Barns *(tel: 822–4593)*, and jumping to create 'an earthquake' at the Observatory *(tel: 822–4593)*.

EAST VANCOUVER AND BURNABY

The rides at **Playland at the PNE** (Pacific National Exhibition) grounds *(tel: 255–5161)* are open from Easter to August. Irresistible attractions include

For youngsters at summer festivals, face painting is serious business

the rollercoaster, log-chute rides, candyfloss and toffee apples. Such quiet pursuits as watching chickens hatch and cows calve during the Pacific National Exhibition in the last two weeks of August are especially interesting to city children.

Toys Plus More, at 6508 Hastings Street *(tel: 298–6970)* offers many delights for kids, ranging from draftboards to G I Joe helicopters and people-sized teddy bears. Shoppers use big black garbage bags to collect purchases. The store is open from Monday to Friday 9.30am–5pm, and on Saturday and Sunday 10am–5pm.

Sports

*V*ancouver is an absolute mecca for sports lovers. The long days of summer are great for golf and tennis; the beaches and sea breezes appeal to swimmers and sailors; there are lots of trails for cyclists and hikers; and local fresh and salt waters teem with life for eager anglers and divers. Even the cold rains of winter do not dampen the spirits of sports lovers, for rain in the city means snow on the mountains for skiers.

LANDSPORTS

BOWLING
When the weather is rainy, the energetic can always seek shelter in one of Vancouver's 20 bowling alleys, some five-pin, some 10-pin. Check the Yellow Pages of the phone book for details of opening times.

BUNGY JUMPING
The sport that New Zealand made famous came quickly to BC. You can jump off a bridge about a 15-minute drive south of Nanaimo at the Bungy Zone *(tel: 753–JUMP)* or call the Bungee Connection *(tel: 736–1975)* and leap from a hot-air balloon or from a 75m crane for the longest step of your life.

CAVING
There are about 2,000 caves in BC, most of them on Vancouver Island. All are in their original natural condition, with no walkways, and only 600 of them have been charted. Popular caves for exploring include the Black Hole (situated in virgin rainforest), the Horne Lake Caves, Paradise Lost and the Artlish River Cave. Contact the BC Speleological Federation at *283–2691* for information.

CYCLING
The Stanley Park Seawall provides the perfect path for an hour of urban cycling. The paved trail following the SkyTrain route from Main Street station to New Westminster is also relatively flat and passes 32 parks and playgrounds. Stanley Park Rentals *(tel: 681–5581)* and other downtown operations rent bicycles by the hour or by the day.

GOLFING
The province's 160 golf courses include 17 in Vancouver open to the public. A letter of introduction from your home club provides entry to private courses. Several par-three courses are scattered throughout the city. Those in Stanley Park *(tel: 681–8847)* and Queen Elizabeth Park *(tel: 874–8336)* are open year-round, but the Ambleside Pitch and Putt *(tel: 922–3818)* has the most spectacular setting.

HIKING AND WALKING
Most major parks in and around Vancouver have well-marked circuits for scenic wilderness hikes and walks. The Stanley Park Seawall is the best walk close to downtown. Serious hikers might want to contact Bear Enterprises *(tel: 847–3351)* in Smithers, who organise hikes through the remote Stikine country in northern BC.

HORSEBACK RIDING

Urban equestrians enjoy the trails at Campbell Park Riding Stables *(tel: 534–7444)* in Langley, which offers both guided and unguided rentals. Riders with more time may want to rough it with wranglers on the range at such working guest ranches as the one at Elkin Creek *(tel: 984–4666)*.

PARAGLIDING

Maxim de Jong, who tried paragliding when it began in the mid-1980s, operates the Mescalito Adventure Company *(tel: 858–2300)* in the Fraser Valley. Paragliders jump off a 15-degree slope and then glide like eagles with the air currents. It takes only a few minutes to set up the harness and canopy and to don the helmet for the flight.

ROCK CLIMBING

In a region with so many mountains, rock climbing is almost an instinct. Learners practise in Lighthouse Park in West Vancouver on cliffs overhanging the water and then move on to tough mountain challenges. Contact the Federation of Mountain Clubs of BC *(tel: 737–3053)* for information.

SKIING

Vancouver's North Shore has three ski areas within a half-hour drive of the city centre. The nearest is Grouse Mountain (1,250m), where in good weather skiers on the Peak, Paradise and Cut runs enjoy spectacular views down to the city centre and across Georgia Strait to the Gulf Islands and Vancouver Island. Cypress Bowl, to the west with its downhill runs, and Mount Seymour, to the east, also offer nordic skiing. Cypress and Grouse are lit for evening skiing until 10pm. All three mountains have equipment rentals

Learning rock climbing opens doors to adventure in a mountainous area like BC

and restaurants. Hemlock Valley, a 2-hour drive east and Whistler/Blackcomb, a 2-hour drive north, are other popular ski areas. Contact Tourism BC at *683–2000* for information.

TENNIS

More than 200 public courts, scattered throughout the city, are free and operate on a first come, first served basis, except for Stanley Park, where there is a court fee in summer. For locations of public courts, call the Parks Board *(tel: 681–1141)*.

Skiing

*Skiers from all
over the world
come to BC*

*More conventional
daytime skiing at Mount
Seymour*

*On the road to
Whistler – top
ski destination*

*One of the two
chairlifts that carry
skiers up the slopes
of Mount Seymour*

BC is one of Canada's top ski playgrounds. The combination of the moderate climate with the proximity of Vancouver airport to good ski facilities, comfortable accommodation and challenging terrain appeals to skiers from around the globe.

When moist, cold air from the Pacific meets the coastal mountains, the result is big flakes of snow which pack the mountain peaks and slopes.

The three North Shore mountains, Cypress, Grouse and Seymour – all within a half-hour drive from Vancouver city centre – offer spectacular sea and city vistas, along with good ski facilities open day and evening from November to April when the snows co-operate.

Japanese skiers have named Whistler/Blackcomb, fast becoming a subject for superlatives all over the world, their favourite ski area, leaving Vail, Chamonix and Zermatt in the shadows. Here, a two-hour

drive north from Vancouver, high-speed quad chairs and other lifts run up spectacular slopes to a variety of gentle runs for novices, alpine chutes, glades, groomed runs, moguls and vast areas of back country for skilled skiers.

Hemlock, in the Fraser Valley, also accommodates overnight guests at its cosy alpine village, and offers 30km of groomed trails. Manning Park Resort is a small family-style ski area at the northern end of the Cascades.

Nordic skiing along trails in the Lower Mainland presents a range of exciting challenges. The 16km of hilly tracks and packed trails at Hollyburn Ridge on Cypress Mountain are open all day and evening until 10pm. The Whistler/Blackcomb area has good groomed trails both on the Valley Trail, traversing the golf course, and at Lost Lake, which features a warming hut for cold days. The Diamond Head area in Garibaldi Park has high glaciers to challenge experts, with an overnight hut available at Elfin Lakes. The Hemlock Valley loop comprises 30km of groomed trails, good for both cross-country and telemark skiing.

Other downhill and nordic ski areas are scattered throughout the BC interior. For the adventurous, there is heli-skiing in the Bugaboos and at Tyax, north of Whistler, and there is snowcat skiing in the Selkirk Mountains.

Night skiing at
Grouse Mountain

WATERSPORTS

Vancouver is surrounded by water on three sides, and BC has more than 7,000km of coastline, 11,000 rivers and creeks, 6,000 lakes, 30 coastal marine parks and countless tidal inlets, offering unmatched opportunities for marine adventure. (See **Getting Away From It All**, pages 128-31.)

CANOEING

Deep Cove Canoe Rentals *(tel: 929–2268,* open in summer only) is a good starting-point for a few hours of paddling around Indian Arm, a wilderness setting a half-hour drive from downtown Vancouver.

FISHING

A fishing licence (saltwater or freshwater, or both), sold in major downtown department stores and in sporting goods shops, is essential. The interior season extends from May to October, while coastal waters may operate year-round. Numerous rivers and lakes contain trout and salmon. Arctic grayling, pike and walleye inhabit northern waters, while the boundary areas contain smallmouth bass and yellow perch. Sturgeon live in the Fraser and Columbia rivers and bass are found on Vancouver Island.

Spring or chinook salmon and coho are the most popular saltwater catches, although some anglers prefer the challenges of sockeye, pink and chum salmon. Coastal waters also harbour halibut, flounder, sole, red snapper, perch, greenling, ling cod and the spotted sea-run cut-throat trout. Such shellfish as abalone, clams, oysters, crabs, mussels, scallops, shrimps and prawns also inhabit these waters. Restrictions concerning size and species are outlined in the *BC Tidal Waters Sport Fishing Guide.*

You can either take a fishing charter, which will look after everything, or you can rent a motorboat. Westin Bayshore Yacht Charters *(tel: 682–3377),* downtown near Stanley Park, and Sewell's Landing Marina in Horseshoe Bay *(tel: 921–7461)* offer both charters and bareboat rentals. For more information, call the Department of Fisheries *(tel: 666–2268).*

KAYAKING

Ecomarine *(tel: 689–7575),* on Granville Island, rents kayaks all year round. A 2-hour rental allows ample time to glide along the quiet waters of False Creek past the market deck, the floating houseboat homes, Science World and the residential community along the south shore. Both one- and two-seater kayaks are available. EcoSummer *(tel: 669–7741)* organises ocean kayak tours through the Gulf Islands, to the killer whale habitat off northern Vancouver Island, and around the Queen Charlotte Islands.

MOTOR BOATING

Canada's largest fleet of self-drive rental boats is moored in Horseshoe Bay, 17km northwest of downtown. Here, Sewell's Landing Marina *(tel: 921–3474)* rents boats by the hour and longer – a great way to explore the coastline and nearby islands.

RIVER RAFTING

In this exhilarating social sport, a dozen or so novices and a couple of expert guides challenge the whitewater. Such Vancouver companies as EcoSummer *(tel: 669–7741)* offer trips varying from a heart-thumping afternoon ride to a two-week cruise through the stunning desert habitat or wilderness rainforest.

SCUBA DIVING

BC's underwater world hides a great diversity of plants and animals, best seen in autumn when plankton and freshwater run-off reach their lowest levels. The submarine jungle includes graceful giant anemones, towering sea-whips, orange sea cucumbers, gorgonian corals, colourful nudibranches, 180 species of sponges and 90 species of sea-stars.

In the waters off Pacific Rim National Park, sometimes called 'the graveyard of the Pacific', dozens of shipwrecks have been found and others are still waiting to be discovered. The 3m-tall bronze mermaid submerged in 18m of water at Saltery Bay near Powell River is a breathtaking beauty. The Diving Locker *(tel: 736–2681)*, Diver's World *(tel: 732–1344)* and Adrenalin Sports *(tel: 682–2881)* organise diving excursions year-round.

SWIMMING

English Bay beaches offer good swimming in summer, but seekers of solitude may prefer Savary Island and Desolation Sound further north, where the waters are just as warm. Saltwater pools at Second Beach in Stanley Park and at Kitsilano Beach are open from June to August. Indoor pools at the UBC Aquatic Centre *(tel: 228–4521)*, the Vancouver Aquatic Centre *(tel: 666–3424)* and the YMCA downtown *(tel: 681–0221)* are open day and evening throughout the year.

An adventure on the water for youngsters at Birkenhead Lake, north of Whistler

A humpback whale tail-thrashing, one of the many species of cetaceans seen off the coast of British Columbia

SPECTATOR SPORTS

WHALE WATCHING

Watching these great mammals of the Pacific is a favourite spectator sport of both residents and visitors. Johnstone Strait, between Vancouver Island and the mainland, is home to the world's largest concentration of killer whales that can be seen on a daily basis.

These sheltered waters, about 400km northwest of Vancouver, are home to 12 pods, totalling approximately 135 killer whales. When conditions permit, you can listen with a hydrophone to orcas emitting their famous songs and clicks. The total killer whale population of BC is around 300.

The whales have a low birth-rate and a low mortality rate. The males may live for up to 50 years, while the females may live twice as long. Johnstone Strait is also home for many sea birds and bald eagles, salmon, seals, sea lions, porpoises, minke whales and humpback whales.

Off the west coast of Vancouver Island, spring is the time to see the big grey whales migrating from Baja California to Alaska. Several companies, such as Bluewater Adventures *(tel. 684–4575)* on Granville Island, organise various whale-watching tours. Bring binoculars.

The California grey whale

TEAM SPORTS

For those who enjoy the roar of the crowd, there are the BC Lions who play home games in the Canadian Football League at BC Place Stadium (777 Pacific Boulevard); the Vancouver Canadians AAA baseball team (one step below major league standard) who perform at Nat Bailey Stadium (33rd Avenue, Ontario Street, adjacent to Queen Elizabeth Park); the Vancouver 86ers soccer team (Swangard Stadium, in Burnaby); and, in winter, the Vancouver Canucks ice hockey team who compete in the National Hockey League in Pacific Coliseum (in Exhibition Park). Information on seasons, game times, venues and tickets is available from the Travel InfoCentre *(tel: 683–2000)*.

HORSE RACING

Horse racing takes place from mid-April to mid-October at Vancouver's

Action-packed rugby union games draw keen spectators in many towns in BC

Exhibition Park *(tel: 254–1631)*. Betting diners can watch the races on closed-circuit television, but the view of Mount Seymour across Burrard Inlet from the stands is so spectacular that it would be a shame to miss it.

The BC Lions football team in action

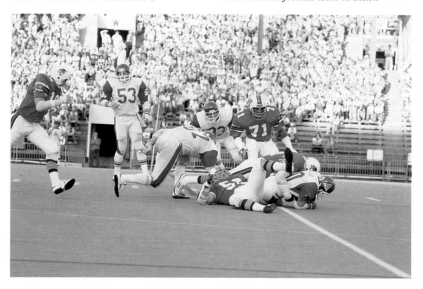

Food and Drink

*E*ast and West meet in Vancouver in an amazing variety of restaurants, some oriental, some European, some African, some North American, and others which artfully combine and innovate to create new cuisines.

Good restaurants of all kinds can be found in the old Gastown district

Fine foods and wines are often found in Vancouver at lower prices than in Europe. Dinner usually costs more than lunch for the same menu, and breakfast is the bargain of the day. Many restaurants are closed on Monday. Except for fast-food places, reservations are recommended for lunch during the week and for dinner on Friday and Saturday evenings. Most restaurants accept major credit cards. Restaurants do not add a service charge, so a tip of between 10 and 20 per cent is welcome.

Restaurants listed here are categorised according to price per person, not including alcoholic beverages:
$: under $5
$$: under $10
$$$: under $20 **and**
$$$$: over $20.

BREAKFAST AND BRUNCH

$$ Chinese dim sum is the best deal in town (see pages 166–7). **Joe's**, at 1150 Commercial Drive (phone number unlisted), serves one of the best cappuccinos in the country. While youths play pool, local radicals, philosophers and yuppies watch television and attempt to solve the problems of the universe. The **Elbow Room Cafe**, at 720 Jervis Street *(tel: 685–3628)*, is trying to keep the bulldozers at bay. The little place, plastered with clippings and photos of the rich and famous, vibrates with the energy of the two owners, who are also the chefs and the waiters.

$$$ For a mellower morning meal, try the classy **Alma Street Cafe**, at 2505 Alma Street *(tel: 222–2244)*, where piano music accompanies Sunday brunch. The buffet brunch at the elegant **Bayshore Garden Lounge**, at 1601 West Georgia Street *(tel: 682–3377)*, offers spectacular scenery combined with fresh and candied fruit, cereals and nuts, meats, eggs, pasta, omelettes, various breads and cheeses and such delicacies as maple crêpes.

ASIAN RESTAURANTS

CHINESE

$$ Many Vancouverites say Szechwan food is finest at **Chongqing**, at Victoria and Broadway *(tel: 254–7434)*, and at the **Moutai Mandarin**, at 1710 Davie Street *(tel: 681–2288)*, both under the same management.

$$$ The **Pink Pearl**, at 1132 East Hastings Street *(tel: 253–4316)*, long the city's best-known Cantonese restaurant, is one of the largest and the best.

$$$$ **Dynasty**, in the New World Harbourside Hotel at 1133 West Hastings Street *(tel: 691–2788)*, features such choice Hong Kong delicacies as shark's fin soup and snake, in a luxurious setting.

$$$$ **Tai Chi Hin**, at 888 Burrard Street *(tel: 682–1888)*, also serves the best in unusual Chinese specialities.

JAPANESE

$ The small **Shogun Sapporo Ramen**, at 518 Hornby Street *(tel: 689–2922)*, serves savoury and substantial portions of garlicky gyoza, steaming ramen, teriyaki, tempura and miso soup.

$$ **Kamei Sushi**, at 1414 West Broadway *(tel: 732–0112)*, and **Shijo**, at 1926 West Fourth Avenue *(tel: 732–4676)*, are both insider's choices for Nipponese specialities.

$$$ The beautifully designed **Koji**, at 640 Hornby Street *(tel: 685–7355)*, is a favourite of downtown business people.

$$$$ **Kamei Royale**, at 1030 West Georgia Street *(tel: 687–8588)*, always adds something special to a longtime favourite menu. At **Suntory**, in the Pan Pacific Hotel at 999 Canada Place *(tel: 683–8201)*, Japanese hostesses in costume serve private feasts.

Oriental cuisine and pleasant décor draw diners to restaurants like the Shabusen

EAST INDIAN

$$$ The **Delta Place Hotel**, at 645 Howe Street *(tel: 687–1122)*, features highly flavoured curries in a daily luncheon buffet.

$$$ **Tandoori King**, at 689 East 65th Street *(tel: 327–8900)*, is patronised by food specialists.

THAI

$$ City restaurateurs like to dine at the **Montri-Thai**, at 2611 West Fourth Avenue *(tel: 738–9888)*.

Ming's restaurant, a dining mecca in
Vancouver's Chinatown

Ming's, the place to go
for dim sum

A mouth-watering
array of dishes in a dim
sum brunch

Dim Sum Brunch

A Sunday-morning crowd slowly moves up a staircase to the second floor, to a cultural experience and fast food at its finest. This is Ming's in Vancouver's Chinatown, one of the biggest and best dim sum restaurants in town.

Dim sum means 'a little bit of heart' in Cantonese, and both Cantonese and other Canadians are eating to their hearts' delight. It is a lively and happy occasion and often a family affair.

Dim sum regulars arrive early and sit near the kitchen for the first choice of freshest food. A procession of little carts, carrying stacks of steaming bamboo baskets and stainless steel containers filled with dozens of different delights, are wheeled among the tables, where hundreds of people are enjoying some of the more than 50 listed delicacies.

Popular dim sum includes *ha gow*, a thin rice dough wrapped around bits of prawns and bamboo shoots and steamed; *cha siu bao*, dumpling-like buns filled with barbecued pork; and sticky rice wrapped in lotus leaves.

Dim sum diners can eat a little or a lot, and pay accordingly. Each portion usually contains two or three bite-sized pieces. The complimentary green jasmine tea or the robust black *bo lei*, goes well with dim sum. When the teapot is empty, simply lift the lid and the waiter quickly refills it. To say thank you, tap your first two fingers on the table. Chinese and local beer also go well with dim sum.

Dim sum restaurants are not renowned for décor, and Ming's is no exception. Arrive early and the place looks bleak. Arrive later, and the animated eaters, the ebony-eyed waitresses and the choreography of the carts in the moveable feast create a splendid scenario. And the noise is a joyful one.

Le Gavroche, though expensive, is one of Vancouver's memorable dining experiences

EUROPEAN RESTAURANTS

$ The **Dutch Pannekoek House**, at 1260 Davie Street *(tel: 669–8211)*, features hearty pancakes rolled like crêpes. This neighbourhood favourite closes at 2.30pm.

$$ The **Swiss Inn**, at 1072 Denman Street (tel: 685–4110), offers great bargains created by a super chef. The **City Bistro**, across from City Hall at 555 West 12th Avenue *(tel: 872–7499)*, sells great hamburgers garnished with potato latkes and sour cream. People in the food business go for Greek food to

Maria's Taverna, at 2324 West Fourth Avenue *(tel: 731–4722)*. The **Old Spaghetti Factory**, at 53 Water Street in Gastown *(tel: 684–1288)*, is a great place to take the kids, offering good family fare.

$$$ **Bandi's Hungarian Restaurant**, at 1427 Howe Street *(tel: 685–3391)*, represents Budapest in all its culinary glory. At **Chez Thierry**, 1674 Robson Street *(tel: 688–0919)*, owner/chef Thierry Damilano serves outstanding country-style French dishes, when he is in the kitchen, and also slices off the top of a champagne bottle with a sword when the mood strikes him. The **Villa del Lupo**, at 869 Hamilton Street *(tel: 688–7436)*, serves timeless Italian cuisine in a Mediterranean setting. Specialities include foccaccia, mushroom mousse, radicchio salad and osso bucco.

$$$$ **Le Gavroche**, at 1616 Alberni Street *(tel: 685–3924)*, is located in the cosy and charming upstairs of an old house (the two window tables offer a great harbour view), and has received several awards for fine cuisine. The food ranges from classic favourite European dishes to mahi mahi and smoked duck. The **Chef & Carpenter**, at 1745 Robson Street *(tel: 687–2700)*, is a neighbourhood French restaurant with two top chefs.

FAST FOOD

Delicatessens, found at most markets and malls, on busy downtown streets and on Commercial Drive, sell cooked meats, cheeses, salads and other snacks from around the world. Although it is rare to find fast food that might please Escoffier, the price is usually reasonable, especially for budget-conscious families with active adolescents.

$ At the **A&W**, at 1103 Denman Street *(tel: 688–1141)*, the bear is sometimes there to greet the kiddies while they eat their burgers. **Burger King**, at 804 Granville Street *(tel: 681–0700)*, makes giant hamburgers. Late-nighters congregate at **Denny's**, at 888 Burrard Street *(tel: 689–3127)*, open 24 hours a day. People go to **Earl's On Top**, at 1185 Robson Street *(tel: 669–0020)*, for the calamari and Caesar salad, as well as the delightful and decorative tropical birds. The **Food Fair** in the Pacific Centre, at Howe and Dunsmuir, sells fast food from many countries and is a good place for watching workers grab a sandwich. The **Fresgo Inn**, at 1138 Davie Street *(tel: 689–1332)*, fills up famished teenagers with big servings of bacon and eggs and hamburgers and chips. **Kentucky Fried Chicken**, at 1147 Davie Street *(tel: 689–1402)*, produces great chicken and coleslaw. Famous for perfect fast food, **McDonald's** has three downtown sites in the Pacific Centre, at 1701 Robson Street and at

734 Thurlow Street. The **White Spot** restaurants, with downtown premises at Georgia and Cardero *(tel: 681–8034)*, Georgia and Seymour *(tel: 662–3066)*, and Robson and Burrard *(tel: 681–4180)*, are BC-owned and almost a local tradition.

$$ The **Cactus Club**, at 1136 Robson Street *(tel: 687–3278)*, is famous for Mexican fajitas and burgers, although the hottest selling items are the decorative papier mâché cows. The latest fast-food outlets on the local scene are Japanese sushi and noodle houses. The **Noodle Express**, at 747 Thurlow Street *(tel: 669–1234)*, is among the best. The **Red Robin**, at 752 Thurlow Street *(tel: 732–4797)*, is a great place to enjoy Mexican food, and overlooks the busiest block on Robson Street.

Reasonably priced fast food is available in the Pacific Centre Mall and other shopping areas in downtown Vancouver

A busy outdoor cafeteria provides quick refreshment at the Plaza of Nations

PLACES TO TALK

$$ **Denny's**, at 888 Burrard Street *(tel: 689–3127)*, is popular with film crews and late-night celebrities. Although the food is fast, the talk is leisurely. The **Hotel Vancouver Lounge**, at 900 West Georgia Street *(tel: 684–3131)* is one of the city's great meeting places. It's relaxed and homely with good daily specials and hamburgers. Writers and publishers love **La Bodega**, at 1277 Howe Street *(tel: 684–8814)*, for the tasty tapas that include the best fried chicken in town, and for the informal Spanish atmosphere and the smiling service. But the **Sylvia Hotel Bar**, at Beach and Gilford *(tel: 688–8865)*, provides the best place to watch the sun set over English Bay.

$$$ **Al Porto**, at 321 Water Street *(tel: 683–8376)*, the home of Umberto's Wine Club, is a good Italian restaurant. The little upstairs dining room is a great place to watch the activities in the harbour while the last rays of the sun colour the North Shore mountains beyond. The **Bayshore Garden Lounge**, in the Bayshore Hotel, at 1601 West Georgia *(tel: 682–3377)*, provides a romantic and comfortable setting looking out on to a lush garden. **Trader Vic's** next door is in South Pacific exotic and cosy style, yet comfortable even when it is packed, which is most of the time. Yuppies congregate at **Joe Fortes**, at 777 Thurlow Street *(tel: 669–1940)*, a good place for people-watching. The **Landing Lounge**, at 374 Water Street *(tel: 688–4800)*, is a romantic spot to try a salmon burger. At the **Monterey Grill Lounge**, in the Pacific Palisades Hotel at 1277 Robson Street *(tel: 684–1277)*, patrons enjoy great food, live music and wickered comfort looking out on Robson Street. The **Pan Pacific Lobby Lounge**,

at 999 Canada Place *(tel: 682–8111)*, provides spectacular views of the Alaska cruise ships and the harbour.

PUBS

There are few traditional British-style pubs in BC, probably because the province is too young and the population too transitory to have traditions. Until the BC government first permitted neighbourhood pubs in the late 1960s, most public drinking was confined to hotels and restaurants.

People who come to Vancouver for the scenery usually prefer such places as the lounge at the ivy-clad **Sylvia Hotel**, at 1154 Gilford Street, where, when conversation lags, the sunset over English Bay compensates. The nearby and more modern **Sands Bayside Lounge**, at 1755 Davie Street, offers an even better view of the bay. **La Bodega**, at 1277 Howe Street, is the closest place to Spain on the continent, and great for an overcast day; drinks can be tempered with tasty tapas of zesty potatoes, fried chicken, sizzling garlic prawns and sausage only a European can make. At another cloistered getaway, **The Rose & Thorne**, at 757 Richards Street, workers, students and business executives read newspapers, play darts, philosophise, and debate love, politics and football fortunes.

Good local brews, usually on tap, include Granville Island and Whistler lagers. The Horseshoe Bay brewery, which, when it opened in 1981, was the first cottage brewery built in Canada in 50 years, also produces a palatable ale.

Generally speaking, the further the watering-hole is from the big city, the friendlier the staff and the clientele. The **Fanny Bay Inn**, built in 1938 near Courtenay on Vancouver Island, is

For a cappuccino and a pastry there are many small cafés in downtown Vancouver

famous for its outdoor patio, oysters, barbecued beef, pork and lamb, cosy fire in the hearth – and the staff, who make visitors feel like locals the first time they visit.

VEGETARIAN FOOD

The **Naam Restaurant**, at 2724 W 4th Avenue *(tel: 738–7151)* is one of the city's most famous vegetarian restaurants, and both the **Buddhist Vegetarian**, at 363 East Hastings Street *(tel: 687–5231)* and **Greens & Gourmet**, at 2681 West Broadway *(tel: 737–7373)* provide good, no-meat meals for the committed.

WEST COAST

$$ The **Only Café**, at 20 East Hastings Street *(tel: 681–6546)*, serves only fish, only perfect, and is the only restaurant in town without a washroom. Halibut is also good at **Bud's Halibut & Chips**, at 1007 Denman Street *(tel: 683–0661)*, a West End hang-out. The **Café Madeleine**, at 3761 West Tenth Avenue *(tel: 224–5558)*, serves no madeleines but excellent sandwiches, a favourite with UBC students. **Fish & Co**, in the Hyatt Hotel at 655 Burrard Street *(tel: 682–3663)*, serves great fresh fish and a fine tomcado salad.

$$$ The **Cannery**, at 2205 Commissioner Street *(tel: 254–9606)*, which specialises in seafood, is built out over the water among warehouses and freighters. The **Salmon House on the Hill**, at 2229 Folkstone Way *(tel: 926–3212)*, offers a spectacular city view on clear days and nights, along with alderwood barbecued salmon. **Delilah's**, hidden beneath the Buchan Hotel at 1906 Haro Street *(tel: 687–3424)*, offers a set-price, two-course and five-course dinner. Diners choose from such dishes as wild mushroom soup and grilled salmon from old railroad-style menus. The **Raintree**, at 1630 Alberni Street *(tel: 688–5570)*, serves such local specialities as sorrel soup, wild greens with edible flowers, braised salmon and mile-high Okanagan apple pie. The **Quilicum**, at 1724 Davie Street *(tel: 681–7044)*, is a simulated Indian longhouse of poles and beams, gravelled walkways and sunken tables, with colourful native masks decorating the walls and recorded Haida folk songs as background music. The chef works at an open grill over an alderwood fire. Specialities include oolichan, bannock bread, caribou, salmon cheeks, wild rice and whipped soap berries.

$$$$ The **Monterey Grill**, in the Pacific Palisades Hotel at 1277 Robson Street *(tel: 684–1277)*, has an award-winning chef who oversees preparation of such favourites as candied salmon, Gulf Island lamb and the best French fries in Vancouver. **Bishop's**, at 2183 West Fourth Avenue *(tel: 738–2025)*, has won numerous awards for such dishes as scallops over citrus fettuccine and steamed mussels.

VICTORIA

Good places to eat in Victoria include **Chandler's** *(tel: 386–3232)*, identified by the big whale mural on an outside wall, a seafood place favoured by many locals. The **San Remo**, at 2709 Quadra Street *(tel: 595–4114)*, which serves Italian and Greek food in a comfortable Mediterranean setting, is a favourite with writers. Reservations are not accepted, but the wait is worth it, as the food and service are excellent. The **Bengal Lounge**, in the Empress Hotel *(tel: 384–8111)*, serves a delicious and inexpensive curry meal in a setting of re-created colonial splendour, with a Bengal tiger guarding the fireplace. The rich pattern of textures includes heavy lace curtains, oriental rugs, rattan chairs, brass and porcelain safari-motif pots of tropical plants, fans hanging from an ornately carved wooden ceiling and a lushly canopied bar.

Rattenbury's, in the Crystal Garden *(tel: 381–1333)*, named to honour the Victorian architect who designed the Empress Hotel and the Parliament Buildings, specialises in West Coast seafood. Locals love **Spinnaker's Brew Pub**, at 308 Catherine Street in Victoria West overlooking the Inner Harbour *(tel: 386–BREW)*. The atmosphere is comfortable and informal. Its features include self-service, terracotta floors with oriental carpets, twin dart boards, historical photos of Victoria on the walls, a good pianist and outdoor waterfront tables in summer. The halibut and chips with Caesar salad is a favourite meal. In-house brews include Spinnaker Ale, Highland Scottish Ale and Empress Stout.

For dessert, buy some chocolate-covered ginger or almond brittle from **Rogers'**, at 913 Government Street *(tel: 384–7021)*, famous for fine candy for

more than a century. More than 20 places in Victoria serve afternoon tea. While the elegant Empress Hotel is the most popular, locals favour **Arthur's**, at 765 Fort Street *(tel: 383–2850, reservations appreciated)*, where the cost is considerably less.

In Victoria, Rattenbury's restaurant is a good place to dine after exploring the shops in the exotic Crystal Garden mall

Hotel Tips

*A*ccommodation in BC ranges from rustic campgrounds to sybaritic suites with views and so many amenities that you never need to leave. Since room size and quality may vary a great deal within one establishment, be specific when making reservations. Reservations are recommended, especially during the crowded days of summer. The Travel InfoCentre, at 1055 Dunsmuir Street, operates a hotel reservation service (tel: 683–2772). Current hotel tax is 17 per cent, but seven per cent is refundable to non-Canadians when total tax paid comes to C$100. For further information, contact the nearest Tourism Canada or BC Tourism Office and request the comprehensive *BC Accommodations Guide.*

DE LUXE HOTELS

Three of Canada's five-diamond CAA/AAA hotels are in Vancouver: the **Four Seasons, Le Meridien** and the **Pan Pacific.** Most have stunning views (request a view room when you reserve), swimming pools, saunas, spas, health clubs, restaurants and bars, lobby shops, concierge, 24-hour room service and valet parking, and most are wheelchair accessible. Rates run from C$150 per room per night. Some hotels offer discounts for families, honeymooners and senior citizens, and for weekly and off-season stays.

De luxe downtown Vancouver hotels include the **Four Seasons,** which sits atop the Pacific Centre's underground mall of 200 shops; the **Hotel Vancouver,** a city landmark which has recently undergone a C$10 million renovation; the **Hyatt Regency** above the Royal Centre Mall; **Le Meridien,** which also manages the spacious apartments in La Grande Residence next door (minimum stay one month); the sparkling **Pan Pacific,** adjacent to the white sails of Canada Place overlooking the harbour; the **Ramada Renaissance,** whose revolving restaurant offers spectacular views especially at sunset; the **Westin Bayshore,** Vancouver's only downtown resort hotel; and the new **Waterfront Centre Hotel** behind the Pan Pacific.

MODERATELY PRICED HOTELS

These hotels, priced from about C$70 for a double room, offer comfortable and clean accommodation and some have mountain and water views. Enquire about discounts when making reservations.

Moderately priced hotels include the **Barclay Hotel,** an 85-room European-style establishment with a licensed lounge and restaurant; the **Blue Horizon,** which has many rooms with panoramic views, private balconies, fridges and coffee-makers; the romantic **Park Royal Hotel** overlooking the Capilano River in West Vancouver, a 15-minute bus ride from the city centre; the **Sunset Inn,** which has 50 condominium suites with kitchens (weekly and monthly rates available); and the **Sylvia Hotel,** an historic brick building overlooking English Bay at the entrance to Stanley Park.

COST-CUTTERS

Several reasonably priced hotels (from about C$50 a double) are found throughout the downtown area. The **Buchan Hotel** rooms have private baths and cable TV, but no phones. The **Kingston Hotel** offers a light complimentary breakfast and a 10 per cent discount for senior citizens and students. The downtown **YMCA** offers good bargains for both single people and couples.

The **Vancouver Youth Hostel** is the only IHF (International Hostelling Federation) establishment in the city. Located in Jericho Beach Park, the 300-bed hostel offers accommodation to anyone, although summer stays are limited to three nights.

The **University of British Columbia** and **Simon Fraser University** offer summer housing from May through to August. Both have single rooms with shared bath, and UBC also has several studio and one-bedroom suites with private bathrooms and kitchenettes.

BED-AND-BREAKFAST ACCOMMODATION

Greater Vancouver has numerous bed-and-breakfast establishments, some luxurious, some spartan, some in urban mansions with en-suite bathrooms and some on rural farms, where everyone joins in to help with the chores – a great way to get to know Canadians. When booking, inquire about such details as whether smoking is permitted, whether credit cards are accepted, and weekly rates. The **Bed & Breakfast Association** is the umbrella organisation for a dozen booking agencies (see page 11 in the *Vancouver Accommodation Guide*), which represent hundreds of

homes in Vancouver, Victoria and Whistler.

CAMPGROUNDS

Several campgrounds are scattered throughout the city, but the **Capilano Mobile Park** in West Vancouver has the most dramatic setting. Early arrivers can pitch their tents right on the east bank of the Capilano River, and English Bay is only a stone's throw away. There are sites for 190 motorhomes and 10 tents. The park has 24-hour-a-day supervision, a TV lounge with video games, the Cedar Room with a 10-person jacuzzi, an outdoor swimming pool and a laundromat.

The glittering new Waterfront Centre Hotel at Vancouver's Canada Place

Practical Guide

Contents

BC Ferries offer an enjoyable way to explore the coastal islands and inlets

ARRIVING
Entry Formalities

Requirements include a valid full passport (except for Americans) and a return or onward ticket, together with evidence of sufficient funds for the duration of your stay. Visas are not required for citizens of Britain, Ireland, Australia, New Zealand and the US. Visitors under 18 years of age unaccompanied by an adult must carry a letter from a parent or guardian granting permission to travel in Canada.

Numerous international airlines serve Vancouver with regularly scheduled flights from Europe, Asia, the South Pacific, the US, Mexico and South America. Vancouver International Airport and Canada Customs and Immigration can be very busy in summer and at Christmas and Easter, so be prepared to wait.

Customs and immigration regulations are strict, and baggage may be searched. Fruit and animal products may not be imported. There is no inbound duty-free shop.

Vancouver Airport is a 30-minute drive from downtown. Taxis from Level II (Domestic Arrivals) cost about C$20 to go downtown. Airport Express buses *(tel: 273–9023)* also leave from Level II every 15 minutes and stop at major downtown hotels and the Greyhound Bus Depot. The cost is about C$10 per person. Passengers en route to Whistler can take the direct Whistler Airport Express Bus, and there are also direct buses to White Rock, Fraser Valley and Surrey (Century Valley Airporter) and Victoria (Pacific Coach Lines).

CAMPING

Camping is a wonderful way to enjoy the fresh air and natural beauty and to make new friends, especially in summer.

There are hundreds of campgrounds in BC, several of them in Greater Vancouver. The Capilano RV Campground *(tel: 987–4722)*, a 10-minute drive across the Lions Gate Bridge from the city centre, is one of the best urban camping areas in the world (see page 175). Suburban campgrounds include the Burnaby Cariboo RV Park *(tel: 420–1722)*, Parks Canada RV Inn *(tel: 943–5811)* in Delta, Richmond RV Park (tel: 270–7878) and KOA Vancouver *(tel: 594–6156)* in Surrey. The campsite at Porteau Cove Provincial Park *(tel: 898–3678)* overlooks Howe Sound, the most southerly fiord in North America. For more information, pick up the *SuperCamping* booklet from any Travel InfoCentre, which lists private campgrounds, BC parks and RV and motorhome dealers.

Regular airline services operate between Vancouver and other airports across BC

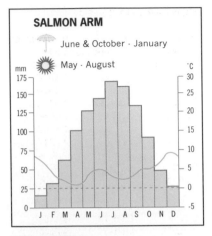

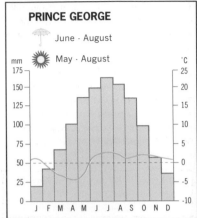

CHILDREN

Vancouver is a great place for a family holiday. Children love the spacious parks and playgrounds to romp and roam. Public transport, whether on planes, trains, buses or ferries, offers reduced fares for youngsters, who particularly enjoy roaming around the decks of the big BC ferries.

Several hotels make an extra effort to cater for kids. Camp Hyatt at the Hyatt Regency in downtown Vancouver *(tel: 800–233–1234 toll-free world-wide)* features reduced room rates, along with special menus for children, both in restaurants and room service. The Camp Hyatt Passport, available to children, aged three to 15, provides puppet shows, films, arts and crafts, sing-alongs and a mid-evening snack on Friday and Saturday. Most major hotels have reliable babysitters.

An abundance of fast-food restaurants such as MacDonald's and Burger King, and such family restaurants as White Spot and Swiss Chalet, have high chairs and special treats for children, to make eating out fun for the family. At Isadora's restaurant on Granville Island, parents can linger over lunch while the children entertain themselves in a small play area inside or at the adjacent water park outside.

For a dizzying array of diversions, track down Chuck E Cheese, at 9898 Government Avenue in Burnaby *(tel: 421–8408; open daily 10.30am–9pm)*, where small bowling-alleys, a ballroom with a deep dive-in-pool of 20,000 coloured balls, a video parlour, various rocket ships and other vehicles for rocking rides, compete with three mechanical orchestras. Most Vancouver attractions offer reduced admission prices for children (see pages 154–5).

CLIMATE

Compared to other cities in Canada, Vancouver and Victoria have a moderate climate, thanks in part to Pacific Ocean currents. There are few extremes in temperature. Vancouver's highest recorded temperature is 33°C and the lowest is -18°C. But clouds and rain can be abundant, especially during the winter months of November, December and

January. While about 100cm of rain fall on Vancouver airport each year, some areas of the North Shore receive as much as 250cm annually. As a rule, the summer months of June, July and August are the driest and sunniest. Monthly hours of sunshine average 305 hours in July and 44 hours in December. For a recorded weather report, call Environment Canada *(tel: 664–9010)*, which also predicts the possibility of rain.

Weather Chart Conversion
25.4mm = 1 inch
°F = 1.8 × °C + 32

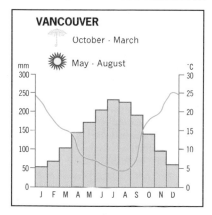

VANCOUVER

October · March

May · August

CONSULATES
Embassies are located in Ottawa, Canada's capital, but consulates in Vancouver include the following:
Australia: 999 Canada Place *(tel: 684–2191)*
Britain: 1111 Melville Street *(tel: 683–4421)*
New Zealand: 701 West Georgia Street *(tel: 684–7388)*
United States: 1075 West Georgia Street *(tel: 685–4311)*

CONVERSION TABLE

FROM	TO	MULTIPLY BY
Inches	Centimetres	2.54
Centimetres	Inches	0.3937
Feet	Metres	0.3048
Metres	Feet	3.2810
Yards	Metres	0.9144
Metres	Yards	1.0940
Miles	Kilometres	1.6090
Kilometres	Miles	0.6214
Acres	Hectares	0.4047
Hectares	Acres	2.4710
Gallons	Litres	4.5460
Litres	Gallons	0.2200
Ounces	Grams	28.35
Grams	Ounces	0.0353
Pounds	Grams	453.6
Grams	Pounds	0.0022
Pounds	Kilograms	0.4536
Kilograms	Pounds	2.205
Tons	Tonnes	1.0160
Tonnes	Tons	0.9842

Men's Suits

UK	36	38	40	42	44	46	48
Rest of Europe	46	48	50	52	54	56	58
US	36	38	40	42	44	46	48

Dress Sizes

UK	8	10	12	14	16	18
France	36	38	40	42	44	46
Italy	38	40	42	44	46	48
Rest of Europe	34	36	38	40	42	44
US	6	8	10	12	14	16

Men's Shirts

UK	14	14.5	15	15.5	16	16.5	17
Rest of Europe	36	37	38 39/40	41	42	43
US	14	14.5	15	15.5	16	16.5	17

Men's Shoes

UK	7	7.5	8.5	9.5	10.5	11
Rest of Europe	41	42	43	44	45	46
US	8	8.5	9.5	10.5	11.5	12

Women's Shoes

UK	4.5	5	5.5	6	6.5	7
Rest of Europe	38	38	39	39	40	41
US		6	6.5	7	7.5	8	8.5

CRIME

Vancouver is still a generally safe city, compared to such vast urban centres as London and New York. Downtown streets are well lit, but caution and commonsense are good watchwords. Hotels recommend placing valuables in their safes. Report any theft immediately to your hotel and the police.

CUSTOMS REGULATIONS

Duty-free allowances for visitors aged 19 and older are 200 cigarettes or 50 cigars or 1kg of tobacco, 1.14 litres of spirits or wine or 24 cans or bottles of beer or ale, and other dutiable goods up to a limit of C$200 in value. There is no duty on personal belongings for use during your visit. Gifts valued at more than C$40 are subject to duty and tax on the excess amount. Any currency carried worth C$5,000 or more must be declared. Revolvers, pistols and fully automatic firearms are prohibited entry into Canada. Quarantine regulations are

BC is crossed by many excellent roads, including the Trans-Canada Highway 1

strict. Plants must be declared and inspected by Agriculture Canada; animals may be quarantined for up to three months. Visitors are only allowed to work in Canada if authorisation was obtained prior to entry into the country.

DISABLED TRAVELLERS

Most major hotels and attractions in Vancouver are wheelchair accessible. For information on facilities for the physically handicapped, contact any Travel InfoCentre, or request the *Easy Going* booklet from the Canadian Paraplegic Association, at 780 Southwest Marine Drive, BC V6P 5Y7 *(tel 324–3611)*.

DRIVING
Breakdowns

The BC Automobile Association honours memberships of other automobile associations around the world. For emergency road service in the Vancouver area, call *293–2222*. Any automobile club card is also valid for discounts at various hotels and attractions. Request the CAA discount when making reservations. For recorded information on highway conditions, call the Ministry of Highways *(tel: 525–4997)*.

Petrol

Petrol (gas) is sold by the litre in regular, premium or super grades, all unleaded. The price of regular per litre is about 60 cents.

Rentals

Renting a car is relatively inexpensive. Major car rental companies include:
Avis *(tel: 682–1621)*
Budget *(tel: 685-0536)*
Hertz *(tel: 688–2411)*
Tilden *(tel: 685–6111)*
A major credit card is required to rent a

car (otherwise a passport, a return ticket and a cash deposit), even if you plan to pay cash. The Visa Gold Card, among others, provides free car insurance; if you are planning to rent a car for a few weeks, it's worth investing in a gold credit card if you qualify. The minimum age to rent a car is 21.

The companies listed, and several others, also rent campervans, motorhomes and four-wheel-drive vehicles. Chauffeured limousines and other vehicles are also available. **Exotic Car Rentals** *(tel: 644–9128)* offers such luxurious vehicles as Porsches, Ferraris and Jaguars. At the other end of the scale is **Rent-A-Wreck** *(tel: 688–0001)*. Rental companies can charge almost double to fill up the tank, so it's better to do it yourself before returning the car.

The sleek Fraser River bridge at Richmond

ELECTRICITY

Canada's electric current is an alternating 110-120 volts and 60 cycles. Adapters, necessary for most overseas appliances, are sold in some hotel shops and at Gulliver's Travels in Park Royal and the Sinclair shopping centres.

EMERGENCY TELEPHONE NUMBERS

Ambulance: *911* or *0* for operator
Dental service: contact your hotel concierge for a recommendation
Emotional Crisis Centre: 733–4111
Fire and rescue: *911* or *0* for operator
Marine and Aircraft distress: 666–4302
Poison Control Centre: *682–5050*
Police: *911* or *0* for operator
Prescription Service: contact your hotel concierge; prescriptions are available only by visiting a Canadian physician
RCMP Freeway Patrol: *911* or *0* for operator
Thomas Cook travellers' cheque refund: 1-800-223-7373 (toll-free).

HEALTH

No vaccinations are required for entry into Canada. Tap water is usually safe to drink. Campers are advised to boil water from lakes and rivers. Canadian health care standards are high. If you become ill, ask your hotel to recommend a nearby physician. Medical insurance to cover the duration of your stay in Canada is essential as medical services are expensive. A visit to a general practitioner costs about C$25, and a day in the hospital C$800. 'Skin So Soft', made by Avon, is the least offensive insect repellent available, and will make travelling in BC back country much more pleasant.

HIRE FACILITIES
Bicycles

Cycling around Stanley Park and other areas of Vancouver is a wonderful way to explore the city and enjoy the sights. Contact Stanley Park Rentals (tel: 681–5581) at the Georgia Street entrance to the park or check the Yellow Pages of the Vancouver telephone directory.

Boats

Sailing boats, motorboats and houseboats are available for rental from dozens of companies both in and outside Vancouver. Contact the nearest Travel InfoCentre for details.

Camping Equipment

Rudy's Sporting Goods, at 3279 West Broadway *(tel: 731–5122)*, rents tents, sleeping-bags, air-mattresses, backpacks, stoves, boots, crampons and other sporting goods.

HITCH–HIKING

Hitch-hiking is not illegal, indeed many backpackers do it, but it is not a recommended form of travel.

Camping on Saltspring Island, with a grandstand view of the island ferries

HOLIDAYS

There are 10 statutory holidays in BC. Banks, post offices, liquor stores, government offices and most other offices and many stores are closed on these holidays. City buses, the SeaBus and the SkyTrain operate on a reduced schedule. Vancouver hotels are rarely fully booked during Canadian holidays, and there are seldom no rooms available during American holidays.

New Year's Day 1 January
Good Friday late March, early April
Victoria Day 24 May or the preceding Monday
Canada Day 1 July
BC Day 1 August
Labour Day first Monday in September
Thanksgiving Day second Monday in October
Remembrance Day 11 November
Christmas Day 25 December
Boxing Day 26 December
Schools are closed during July and August, for 10 days in March or April for the Easter or spring break, and for two weeks in late December/early January for the Christmas holidays.

INSURANCE

Any medical, baggage or other personal insurance should be purchased before leaving home. Any vehicle rental automatically includes third-party-liability insurance for damage to people and property. Loss and damage insurance, which covers the rental car, costs extra, as do personal accident insurance and personal effects coverage for the driver and passengers.

LANGUAGE

English is the language of business in BC. However, thanks to the native

Indians and continuing waves of immigrants from Europe, Asia and around the world, many other languages, ranging from Chinook to Vietnamese, are also spoken. Canadian English has been most influenced by Americans, primarily through the media and advertising. Following are a few words familiar to British Columbians, but foreign to many visitors:

Anglophone	English-speaking person
bannock	Indian bread
bar	a ridge of sand or gravel in a stream or river where gold may be found by panning, but also a drinking place
First Nations	native Indian people
Inuit	Eskimo
Mountie	RCMP officer
potlatch	a native Indian festival
saltchuk	ocean
sushi	cold Japanese appetisers, made from raw fish and cooked rice

Evening crowds at Canada Place can enjoy the sunset from the public promenade

LOST PROPERTY

Vancouver has two lost property centres: BC Transit (bus, SkyTrain losses) *tel: 682–7887*, and Police (lost property rooms) *tel: 665–2232*. Otherwise check with the nearest police station or call the head office of the company.

MAPS

Maps of Vancouver and BC are available from any Travel InfoCentre.

MEDIA

Newspapers and magazines

The best daily in the country, the morning *Globe & Mail,* has limited local news. However, *The Province*, a tabloid, and *The Vancouver Sun*, a broadsheet, both morning papers, cover city news and events. All three are available at news-stands and in street coin boxes. The weekly *Westender* (published on Thursdays) provides compact coverage of entertainment and other downtown events, and is available free at most hotels. The monthly *WHERE Vancouver* is also available in hotels at no charge and for a dollar in coin boxes at the SeaBus Terminal. It is designed especially for visitors and includes information on shopping, dining, attractions, entertainment, special events, maps and evening television programmes. Such local glossy monthly magazines as *Vancouver* and *Western Living* include articles of local interest.

The ground hog, or marmot, ever alert for preying eagles, inhabits high pastures

Radio and television

Favourite local radio stations include CBC at 690 AM and 105.7 FM (talk and classical music with no commercials); CKNW 980 (talk, middle-of-the-road music and sport); CHQM at 1320 AM (memory music); and 103.5 FM (contemporary music).

Local television stations include CBC-TV (Canadian Broadcasting Corporation) on Cable 3; BCTV (the CTV network) on Cable 11; and the Knowledge Network (the BC educational channel) on Cable 5 (no commercials). Dozens of other channels, including PBS, ABC, CBS and NBC from the US, are also available locally. Check the listings at the back of *WHERE Vancouver* magazine.

MONEY MATTERS
Currency

Canada has a decimal currency system with 100 cents to the dollar. Coins are one cent, five cents (a nickel), 10 cents (a dime), 25 cents (a quarter) and the one-dollar coin called a Loonie (because of the loon bird on one face). The bills (notes) are colour-coded: $2 is brown, $5 is blue, $10 is purple, $20 is green, $50 is red and $100 is beige. Merchants seem reluctant to give up a lot of change, so $100 bills are not popular. $20 bills are always acceptable. Thomas Cook travellers' cheques denominated in Canadian or US$ are a secure and convenient way of carrying larger amounts of money and can be used as cash in most hotels and restaurants.

Money Exchange

Most foreign currencies and travellers' cheques can be exchanged at the foreign exchange counters at the airport, at major city banks and hotels, and at the following Thomas Cook Foreign Exchange locations:

1016 West Georgia Street, Vancouver;
999 Canada Place, Suite 130 (Pan Pacific Hotel Entrance), Vancouver;
Eaton Centre Metrotown, 2193A, 4700 Kingsway, Burnaby;
1111 Guildford Town Centre, Surrey.

These branches will cash Thomas Cook travellers' cheques free of commission and provide emergency assistance in cases of loss or theft of Thomas Cook travellers' cheques.

Since exchange rates fluctuate, check the Canadian dollar rates upon your arrival in Canada.

Credit Cards, such as American Express, Carte Blanche, Diners Club, MasterCard and Visa, are widely accepted in hotels, restaurants, shops and parking lots.

Taxes

The federal GST (Goods and Services Tax) is currently seven per cent. However, foreign visitors to Canada may claim a rebate when purchases total more than C$100. Pick up a rebate form at the nearest Travel InfoCentre, or call toll-free *1-800-668-4748* for further details. BC provincial sales tax is six per cent on most merchandise, hotel tax is 17 per cent including the seven per cent GST and there is a 10 per cent sales tax added to liquor consumed in bars and restaurants.

OPENING TIMES

Banks Major banks downtown open at 8am. Some banks are open on Saturday morning, but all are closed on Sundays and holidays. Normal banking hours are 10am–4pm Monday to Friday, often extending to 5pm on Friday.

Museums, galleries and attractions Most are open daily 10am–5pm, but some are closed one day a week, and some have extended or shortened hours on certain days.

Post Offices are open Monday to Friday 8.30am–5.30pm. Some sub-offices are open Saturday mornings, and postal counters in 7-Eleven stores are open until 11pm.

Shops Most shops and stores are open Monday to Friday 9.30am–6pm, with hours extended to 9pm on Thursday and Friday. Most are open Saturday 9.30am–5.30pm, and many are open on Sunday, noon–5pm. Such convenience stores as 7-Eleven are often open 7am–11pm and some are open all night.

PERSONAL SAFETY

Although Canada's wildlife ranges from polar bears to mammoth mosquitoes, Vancouver's animals are limited to squirrels, racoons and an occasional mosquito. The North Shore mountains are home to deer, coyotes and black bears. If you see a bear, talk quietly and then back off slowly! The bear will likely amble off in search of more berries in a more serene setting. The only real hazard in Vancouver is rain, which tends to dampen spirits and make sightseeing a little soggy.

PHARMACIES

Medical prescriptions in BC are available only through a local physician. Many pharmacies are hidden at the back of big drugstores, which entails navigating through aisles of various and sundry goods. These drugstores sell all kinds of non-prescription medicines, along with contraceptives, insect repellent, vitamins, tissues, and a host of other items. Shoppers Drug Mart, at 1160 Robson Street *(tel: 681–8177)*, and London Drugs, at 1187 Robson Street *(tel: 669–7374)*, are open from Monday to Saturday 9am–10pm and on Sunday 10am–8pm.

PHOTOGRAPHY

Print film, which is inexpensive and sold almost everywhere, can be developed within an hour or two at numerous photo shops. Slide film, sold primarily in photo shops, takes 24 hours to develop, except for Kodachrome, which takes a week. CustomColor, at 1110 Robson Street *(tel: 681–2524)*, provides a reliable service for both prints and slides. Many shops sell disposable cameras.

PLACES OF WORSHIP

The many places of worship representing the various denominations and faiths in and around Vancouver include the following:
Akali Singh Sikh Temple, *1890 Skeena Street (tel: 254–2117)*
Beth Israel Synagogue, *4350 Oak Street*

(tel: 731–4161)
Canadian Memorial United Church,
1811 West Sixteenth Avenue (tel: 731–3101)
Central Presbyterian Church, *1155 Thurlow Street (tel: 683–1913)*
Christ Church Anglican Cathedral, *690 Burrard Street (tel: 682–3848)*
Christian Science Church, *1160 West Georgia Street (tel: 685–7544)*
First Baptist Church, *969 Burrard Street (tel: 683–8441)*
Holy Rosary Catholic Cathedral, *464 Richards Street (tel: 682–6774)*
Ismaili Mosque, *4010 Canada Way, Burnaby (tel: 438–4010)*

POLICE

The RCMP (Royal Canadian Mounted Police) cover areas where there is no municipal police force. Call 911 or 0 for the operator for any emergencies.

Lawn bowling is a popular sport among more energetic senior citizens

POST OFFICES

The main post office at 349 West Georgia Street is open from Monday to Friday 8am–5.30pm. Many sub-offices in malls, drugstores, convenience stores and even dry-cleaning shops are also open on Saturday as well. Most offer postage, courier and facsimile (fax) services. Stamps are also sold at the front desk in some hotels and in tourist shops which sell postcards. Canada Post boxes are red. Mail can be received 'c/o General Delivery' at any post office in Canada. To send a telegram, call Unitel on *681-4231.*

SENIOR CITIZENS

Seniors are getting younger every day. The term 'seniors' or 'pensioners' used to mean anyone aged 65 or 'better', but now numerous transport and tour companies, hotels, stores, attractions and events are offering reduced rates to people as young as 50. Carry an ID card or any other official document that indicates your birth date.

The Hyatt, Park Royal and Westin Bayshore hotels, among others, offer senior discounts. Many local restaurants give 10 to 20 per cent discount to seniors, while others offer small-portion meals and early-bird specials. Watch for advertised specials in local newspapers and on menus, or enquire upon entering any restaurant.

Domestic airlines, the harbour and Granville Island ferries, city transport including the SeaBus and SkyTrain, and BC Rail all offer reduced fares to seniors. Call the company directly for details. Such attractions as the Vancouver Aquarium, the Dr Sun Yat-sen Chinese Garden, the Vancouver Art Gallery, the Museum of Anthropology, the Maritime Museum, Science World, the IMAX show, the Bloedel Conservatory and Grouse Mountain offer reduced admission prices to seniors. The Vancouver Aquatic Centre offers a seniors' programme which includes exercises on the deck and in the pool, and organises day trips outside the city and such special events as Valentine Tea.

City cinemas, theatres and the symphony offer reduced rates to seniors, sometimes by as much as 50 per cent.

Ask about discounts also while shopping. Some supermarkets, drugstores and department stores reduce prices by 10 to 15 per cent one day a month for seniors.

Travel-wise seniors get great holiday bargains through Elderhostel at 33 Prince Arthur Avenue, Toronto, Ontario M5R 1B2. This organisation sells dozens of different action and study trips throughout BC, including the Gulf Islands, Strathcona Park and Salmon Arm. A monthly publication, *Today's Times (tel: 683–1344)*, is geared especially to the needs of senior readers.

STUDENT AND YOUTH TRAVEL

Many attractions and events in the Vancouver area offer reduced rates for students. Bring your student card.

TELEPHONES

Public telephones can be found in post offices, hotel lobbies, public buildings and in phone booths on various streets throughout the city. Local calls cost 25 cents for an unlimited time. Some public phones are specifically for long-distance calls and some are designated for credit card use only. Both local and international calls are usually more expensive on hotel phones. Call 0 for the operator to enquire about discounts for dialling both domestically and abroad at

certain times. The area code for BC is *604*.

International calls can be dialled direct using the following codes: Britain is *01 44*, Ireland *01 353*, Australia *01 61* and New Zealand *01 64*. Drop the initial 0 before dialling the area code and the number. For calls to other provinces of Canada and to the US, dial 1, the area code and the number.

TICKET AGENCIES

For such events as opera, symphony, ballet, theatre, sports, rock concerts and some attractions, call Ticketmaster on *280–4444*. By telephone you can pay by American Express, MasterCard or Visa. At counters scattered throughout city shopping malls, you can pay by credit cards or cash. Cinema tickets are sold only at individual theatres. For programme times at Cineplex Odeon, call *687–1515*.

TIME

Most of BC is on Pacific Standard Time, which in summer is nine hours behind GMT. Clocks are put back an hour on the last Sunday in October, and an hour forward on the first Sunday in April, for daylight-saving time. Vancouver time is the same as California, three hours behind Toronto and New York. For most of the year, Vancouver is 18 hours behind Sydney and 21 hours behind Auckland.

TIPPING

Tips generally range from 10 to 20 per cent in restaurants and bars and for taxis. A higher tip should reflect better service. There is no need to tip when the service is substandard. Tipping is optional for porters, doormen, chambermaids and other service personnel.

*Trips aboard BC's coastal ferries afford
spectacular views of the many islands*

TOILETS

Public toilets are found in railway and
bus terminals, shopping centres and
department stores. If you are desperate
and there are no public toilets around, a
hotel, bar, or restaurant will sometimes
let you use its facilities.

TOURIST OFFICES

For brochures, maps, and other
information on Vancouver and BC,
contact the following:
UK: Tourism BC, *1 Regent Street,
London S1Y 4NF (tel: 930–6857)*
US: Tourism BC, *2600 Michelson Street,
Irvine, California 92715 (tel: (714)
852–0168)*
Australia: Tourism Canada, *AMP
Centre, 50 Bridge Street, Sydney NSW,
Australia 2000 (tel: 231–6522)*
**New Zealand: Canadian High
Commission,** *ICI House, 67 Molesworth
Street, Wellington, New Zealand (tel:
739–577).*
Branches of Thomas Cook Travel can
also book items such as sightseeing tours
and car hire. The branches most likely to
be used by incoming travellers are:
1155 Robson Street, Vancouver and in
Eaton's at: Pacific Centre, 701 Granville
Street, Vancouver

200-2929 Barnet Highway, Port
Coquitlam
Lansdowne Mall, 8311 Lansdowne
Road, Richmond
Victoria Eaton Centre, Victoria.

TOURS

Visitors to Vancouver can take to the
water aboard the SeaBus or the Granville
Island and BC ferries, in a canoe or
kayak, or on a motorboat or yacht.
Landlubbers can tour on foot and by
bicycle, antique car, bus or limousine.
Some visitors take to the air in sea-
planes, gliders, helicopters and hot-air
balloons. Although North American
travellers tend to be do-it-yourself
sightseers or rely on friends and relatives,
numerous commercial tours are
available, especially in summer. Many
can be pre-booked within your overall
travel plan, or booked at the Thomas
Cook Travel offices listed on this page.
The booklet *Sightseeing Tours &
Transportation,* stocked at Travel
InfoCentres, is helpful.

Bicycle Tours

The Bicycling Association of British
Columbia *(tel: 731–7433)* is the umbrella
organisation for several cycling clubs
including the Vancouver Bike Club,
which welcomes non-members to join in
city cycling and tours further afield for
both leisurely wheeling and technical
training camps.

Bus and Car Tours

Gray Line *(tel: 681–8687)* and Pacific
Coach Lines *(tel: 662–7575),* among
others, offer various sightseeing tours,
with itineraries ranging from a city circle,
similar to the Trolley Tour (see pages
32–3), and an evening dinner tour (a
great way to meet fellow travellers) to a

seven-day return ride through the Rockies to Calgary. Early Motion Tours *(tel: 687–5088)* offer the luxury of a finely tuned original 1928 or 1930 Model A Ford phaeton convertible. The driver, former teacher 'Fridge' Fridulin, provides a continuous commentary on city sights and a Polaroid photograph of you and the phaeton as a souvenir. Classic Limousine Service *(tel: 669–5466)* creates tailored tours in the luxury of a limousine, day or night year-round.

Historical Walking Tours
Local historian Chuck Davis *(tel: 583–2920)*, who probably knows Vancouver past and present better than anyone, designs walking tours of the city centre to meet your requirements.

Train Tours
Harbour Tours *(tel: 688–7246)* offer a ride back in time aboard the historic Royal Hudson steam train to Squamish, with an optional return aboard the MV Britannia, from June to mid-September.

Water Tours
Gray Line *(tel: 681–8687)* and the SS *Beaver (tel: 682–7284)* offer harbour sightseeing excursions. The SS *Beaver* tour of Indian Arm includes a mesquite-grilled salmon lunch. Both Gray Line and the SS *Beaver*, along with Bayshore Yacht Charters *(tel: 682–3377)*, offer three-hour dinner cruises in which salmon and a spectacular sunset are likely to feature in the evening meal. Both Bayshore Yacht Charters and Sewell's Landing Marina *(tel: 921–7461)*, in Horseshoe Bay, offer skippered fishing tours. For whitewater adventure from May to September, contact Hyak Wilderness Adventures *(tel: 734–8622)*,

who guided staff of the *National Geographic* down the Chilko and Chilcotin rivers. The company's Rapids Transit System runs from downtown Vancouver to the Chilliwack, Thomson and Chilko rivers, where the intrepid go with the flow of rushing whitewater in inflatable rafts or kayaks.

TRANSPORT
Airlines
Air BC & Air Canada *(tel: 688–5515)*
Canadian Airlines *(tel: 279–6611)*
Harbour Air *(tel: 688–1277)*
Helijet Airways *(tel: 273–1414)*
Tyee Airways *(tel: 689–8651)*
Vancouver Helicopters *(tel: 525–1484)*

Buses
Airport Express *(tel: 273–9023)* operates between the airport and downtown.
Cascade Bus Lines *(tel: 662–7953)* runs to the Fraser Valley.
Gray Line *(tel: 681–8687)* offers sightseeing tours.

Bus tours and sea cruises are among the many options available to BC's visitors

Greyhound *(tel: 662–3222)* operates throughout Canada.

Whistler Express *(tel: 273–9023)* runs to Whistler.

BC Transit *(tel: 261–5100)*, Vancouver's regional public transport system, includes buses, the SeaBus and the SkyTrain, which run along major arteries through the city centre and suburbs.

There are three fare zones in Greater Vancouver. Day passes are available for children, adults and senior citizens. Exact change in coins is preferred, but tickets and passes are sold at 7-Eleven and at other convenience stores and drugstores.

Transit timetables are available from public libraries, city and municipal halls, Travel InfoCentres and BC Transit offices and terminals. For Blue Bus routes and schedules from downtown to West Vancouver, call 985–7777.

The SeaBuses, which are actually 400-passenger catamaran ferries, make the 15-minute trip across Burrard Inlet to North Vancouver every 15 minutes. Although they have no outside decks, the views are still spectacular. The SkyTrain runs 22km from Canada Place downtown to Scott Road, beyond New Westminster, with 14 stops en route. Most of the line is elevated, so the trip is scenic when the sun is shining. Trains run every five minutes at an average speed of 75km per hour.

Ferries

The little Aquabus Ferries operating from the foot of Hornby Street and the False Creek ferries from the Aquatic Centre make the five-minute run to and from Granville Island seven days a week year-round.

BC Ferries *(tel: 685–1021)* carry both vehicles and foot-passengers and run from Tsawwassen (an hour's drive south from the city centre) to Swartz Bay (a half-hour from Victoria) and Nanaimo on Vancouver Island and to the Gulf Islands.

From Horseshoe Bay (a half-hour drive northwest from downtown Vancouver), ferries sail regularly to Nanaimo, Bowen Island and the Sunshine Coast.

Taxis

It's hard to hail a cab in downtown Vancouver, especially in the pouring rain when you need one most. It's best to head to the nearest big hotel, where taxis usually wait in line, or to call one of the following cab companies:

Black Top *(tel: 681–2181)*
MacLures *(tel: 683–6666)*
Yellow Cab *(tel: 681–1111)*

Trains

BC Rail *(tel: 984–5246)* operates a daily round-trip rail service from North Vancouver via Whistler to Lillooet, and trains three times a week to Prince George via 100-Mile House, Williams Lake and Quesnel. VIA Rail *(tel: 800–561–8630)* operates a thrice-weekly passenger service across Canada, departing from the station on Main Street opposite the Science Centre.

VIA Rail's luxury trans-Canadian train, the 'Silver and Blue', runs from Toronto to Vancouver and can be booked outside Canada. So can the privately run 'Rocky Mountaineer', running from Vancouver through Jasper and Banff to Calgary.

Summer tours with the Great Canadian Railtour Company (tel: 800–665–7245) from Vancouver to Banff and Jasper are especially popular.

ACKNOWLEDGEMENTS
The Automobile Association wishes to thank the following photographers and libraries for their assistance in the preparation of this book.

Peter Timmermans was commissioned to take all photographs not mentioned below. (Zefa Picture Library (UK) Ltd.)

BRITISH COLUMBIA TOURISM p158a Skiing, 163b B C Lions football team
IMAGE FINDERS PHOTO AGENCY INC p120a Lady Rose ferry (Bob Herger), on the deck of the Lady Rose (Boulter–Wilson), p121b Grenville Channel (Bob Herger)
NATURE PHOTOGRAPHERS LTD p105 bald eagle (James Hancock), p162a humpback whale (Paul Sterry), p162b California gray whale (Paul Sterry)
SPECTRUM COLOUR LIBRARY p135b the Bow River with CPR track
The remaining photographs belong to the Automobile Association's own photo library (AA PHOTO LIBRARY) and were taken by Michael Dent.
Pages 2, 16, 67, 68, 92, 96, 97, 98c, 137 169.

The Automobile Association would also like to thank Peter Trower for the use of his poem *The Alienating*, and Bruce I Burnett for *A Run Through Stanley Park*.